donated by: Dave Helseth

with

School/Site Planning

by

Howard J. Feddema, Ed.D.

ACKNOWLEDGMENTS

―――――――――

This book is dedicated, with deep gratitude,
to the over 700 school districts and educational systems and
more than 4500 program graduates that have validated the strategic
planning process and discipline described in this book and who have
contributed immeasurably to my own understanding
and appreciation of Strategics®.

and to

Judy Wallace Cook

Contents

Preface

It seems that Solomon exceeded even his own wisdom when he observed, "Of the making of books, there is no end." I now think he meant that an author never finishes one. No sooner is it published than it begins to cry out, rather shamefacedly, for correction, revision, and updating. Such is the case with *Strategic Planning for America's Schools*.

When this book was first published in 1986, it represented the best of my thinking for the times. Well, the times certainly have changed—in ways even more dramatic and more unprecedented than the book suggested. And, thanks to many friends and colleagues, I and my associates have had unparalleled opportunities to learn even more about a craft we thought we had mastered years ago.

When we introduced strategic planning to educational clients over two decades ago, our early attempts to more-or-less adapt the corporate planning method to education were, upon reflection, somewhat amateurish, perhaps a bit naive. The basic approach in terms of philosophy, intent, and scope was right, but it needed the tempering that only actual field experience can provide. Over the years our planning system has matured to the point that it is generally recognized as state-of-the-art strategic planning for education. It has been adopted, adapted, and imitated by accreditation agencies, state departments of education, and free lance planners. That achievement is not without reason: it is still the only strategic planning system specifically developed within and for education. Of the planning system's twenty components, eighteen have been either invented or redefined by my associates and I to accommodate the special needs and circumstances of educational organizations.

This kind of advancement in strategic planning would not have been possible without the good grace of over seven hundred school districts and numerous other educational groups with whom we have worked. In 1989, the American Association of School Administrators (AASA) and my firm, The Cambridge Group, joined in a partnership to create the International Strategic Planning Center for Education®.

This was a very logical and quite appropriate development since it was AASA who provided me the very first opportunity to bring strategic planning to educational groups. This partnership has provided us an expansive range of experiences, from training over a thousand internal planning facilitators in AASA certification programs to being in a position, through AASA, to influence significantly national educational reforms. Through the Planning Center, now exclusively directed by Cambridge, we have also created formal partnerships with state associations of school administrators and school boards, which not only have involved us in state and local planning efforts, but also have given us a deeper understanding of the special nature of each state's educational needs and aspirations. In recent years, these partnerships have afforded us the opportunity to work with state governments and to actually influence legislation.

In addition, we have active partnerships with The Association for the Advancement of International Education and International School Services. Through these agencies, we have provided strategic planning facilitation and training for international schools around the world. My associates and I are sincerely grateful to all of you who have participated in and supported our attempt to bring the best strategic planning to America's schools. We think that you have succeeded in making us the premier planning organization in the nation. That is an honor that carries with it a commensurate responsibility. That is why we are committed to continue to learn about planning, to improve our skills with every plan we direct, and to share with you what our experiences teach us.

This edition of *Strategic Planning for America's Schools*, however, is more than another printing: It contains significant revisions in both the process and discipline as well as original essays pertaining to the nature and scope of strategic planning. For example, here I differentiate strategic planning—both by context and content—from other ordinary kinds of planning such as comprehensive, long-range, program, and project planning. Also, I try to make it clear that true strategic planning is not just a simple one-dimensional methodology, but that strategic planning must deal with strategic issues in strategic ways. In the same vein, I, along with Howard Feddema, explain the relationship of "site-based" or "school-based" planning to strategic planning and attempt to provide a comprehensive guide to school strategic planning. We think that this subject is especially pertinent because of the emphasis being placed on "site-based" planning by so many state reform measures and because of the apparent confusion on the part of both legislators and administrators over the kind of planning suitable and possible for individual schools. Furthermore, our school planning process and discipline serve to exceed all of the requirements of accreditation agencies, state departments of education, "school improvement" planning, Title I Compliance, and all local board initiatives.

Besides these additions, we have made significant improvements in both the process and discipline. For example, "objectives" have been redefined and narrowed to a "bottom line" concept of student achievement or student success. The planning team has been reconstructed to assure credibility, and a new emphasis is placed both on the development of the action plans as well as on communicating the plan to all publics.

But the really significant changes are in matters that pertain to the nature of the organization itself. It may seem subtle, but we now know that "participatory management" is an oxymoron, a kind of self-delusion. Further, we believe that management itself is rapidly becoming obsolete. So we have dropped all references to participatory management, and have recast our decision-making activity in something we call *Whole-Context Organization™*. We like the concept so much, we have registered the term. The major impacts of this new approach are that we spend more time up front in an examination of organizational capacity, and the entire implementation phase is completely redesigned consistent with *Whole-Context Systems™*. All this is consistent with the courses we now teach in *strategic thinking, strategic planning, strategic action, strategic organization,* and *site planning.*

As a special feature of this edition, we have included several essays on strategy. These were written as occasional pieces, but together, I trust, constitute a philosophical, albeit practical, context for the remainder of the book.

All this and more combine to make our planning and organizational development system now much better than it was before. Our solemn promise to you is to continue to make what we believe is the best approach to creating strategic educational systems even better.

WJC

CHAPTER ONE

TOWARD A PHILOSOPHY OF PLANNING

A Question of Planning

Sir Winston Churchill, from time to time, observed that the process of all human and natural events works somewhat like a formula:

$$PAST \times PRESENT = FUTURE$$

That is to say, the past, as it conflicts or interacts with the present produces the future.

Maybe so. But there is another possibility. Suppose the proposition is stated in this fashion:

$$PAST \times FUTURE = PRESENT$$

Does it make a difference? The answer is a double affirmative.

How Things Happen

First, it makes a difference in our perception of *how* things happen. The Churchillian view is that of the historian. Essentially, it holds that whatever happens is, at best, the result of coincidence; at worst, accident. The emphasis is on holding together the past with the present; on interpreting the past through the present; and on finding some logical, sequential connection, if not evolution, in the events of the past to the circumstances of the present. That assimilation when it is projected systematically forward, becomes the future. Such a rationale is the basis of the theory of natural selection, the Newtonian view of the universe, the Hegelian dialectic, Scientific Organizational Theory, "Management By Objectives," and long-range planning as practiced by most American companies.

The second view is that of the futurist. It sees the future not as an accident or coincidence, but as the result of events and actions, which, in their own present time, imbued intrinsic purpose beyond themselves. The future actually casts its shadow backward, and is realized gradually in the present—albeit never exactly or completely as visualized. The present thus becomes the eternal quest of the future. In a real sense, the present is nothing but the future chasing itself. That means that the true futurist recognizes that the future is always realized, intentionally or not, in the present tense. It's never postponed. Emphasis is on the here and now; on today's achievement. That is the philosophy underlying most western religions, Manifest Destiny, the American space program, championship football teams, breakthrough enterprises of all kinds, and revolutionaries.

Why Things Happen

Second, it makes a difference in our conception of *why* things happen. The historian's formula recognizes cause and effect relationships but concentrates primarily on the effects. Events become the result of the whims and follies of humankind and the phenomena and quirks of nature—all combined with the eternal vagaries of luck, fate, chance and, from time to time, magic. Because there is no control, planning—or, for that matter, hop —is rendered irrelevant. The only choice is no choice. The only action possible is reaction; and response is ultimately translated into the wringing of hands or the beating on of pans in desert places. This notion is the basic presupposition of behaviorism, most Eastern religions, governmental bureaucracy, *laissez-faire* economics, and "Management By Walking Around," as it once occurred to Tom Peters.

On the other hand, the futurist's formula places the emphasis on cause rather than effect. It holds that, although some things themselves are beyond control, none of those things control people who choose to design and build according to their own purpose. The future is thus shaped, molded, created by the genius of human invention. And, the application of human energies. For that reason, emphasis is on objective criteria by which progress can be measured, with corresponding measurement being made of each factor and person contributing to the progress. This is the fundamental premise of medical science, real free enterprise, military campaigns, competitive sports, and strategic planning as practiced early on by Moses.

The True Futurist vs. the Pop Futurist

The strategic planner is by definition a futurist—a true futurist. Please understand, the strategic planner is not a "pop" futurist—that strange breed of prophet *cum* charlatan that has dominated the quasi-intellectual circles in recent years and, regretably, seems now to be exerting perilous influence even on legitimate planners. Evidently, "pop" futurism became in the decade of the nineties just another faddish dalliance such as the "pop" sociology of the sixties (*The Catcher in the Rye*); "pop" psychology of the seventies (*I'm OK; You're OK*); and "pop" management of the early eighties (*The One Minute Manager*). To be sure, the prophecies about the new millennium are usually entertaining and quite often very persuasive, providing amazingly minute detail of that brave new world: a global econocomputerelectronikinetecologistic egalitacracy known mostly for its swinging economies and swaying demographics. These are the optimistic prophecies. Others, the proverbial prophets of doom, gallop wildly about on the four horses of the Apocalypse and scare the living hell out of people.

Both kinds of "pop" futurists are dangerous because of the insinuation — if not actual declaration—they make about the relationship people, organizations, and institutions bear to their future. There are two primary dangers arising from "pop" futurism, and both are exactly counter in principle to even the idea of strategic planning. The first danger is that prophecies of any kind have a way of becoming self-fulfilling. That is to say, any notion, no matter how far-fetched, if accepted through general familiarity, soon is allowed to become a present reality. Other possibilities, hypotheses or options are never considered. Creation and challenge give way to acquiescence. It is that rationale which discourages planning of any kind. After all, *que sera sera.*

The second danger is that the person is negated as a potential change-agent. Things happen in and of themselves; therefore, the proper role for human beings is one of either mere behavioral response or detached philosophical observation. That is why the "pop" futurists urge "preparation *for* the future," rather than "preparation *of* the future." It is this rationale that has typically attempted something called "long-range planning," which was usually nothing more than a collection of SWAG projections accompanied by some SWAG reactions. In this kind of "planning," there is never any hint of control over outcomes—certainly not over the future. It is nothing more than anticipatory acquiescence.

In effect, the "pop" futurist is an anachronistic historian, recording the future as a *fait accompli*. The only difference between the historian and the "pop" futurist is that one concocts system from guess and supposition; the other embellishes guess and supposition with system. But the strategic planner—the true futurist—believes that the future is yet to be made, and that it will be exactly what people make it. Ironically, by acting on this simple belief, the strategic planner creates history.

A Case in Point

Recently, a national education association published what is at once both the most succinct and the most comprehensive list of prophecies about the schools of the future. This matter-of-fact description of the future seems to represent the state-of-the-art thinking among educational leaders. The twelve predictions for the future of the nation's schools include:

1. As standards rise, schools will be expected to develop individual education for all students. The effect of the standards will be monitored not only in terms of student success, but also in terms of dropout rates and equity concerns. Schools will try to identify student problems during the first six weeks of the school year and provide immediate counseling, as needed, to help students succeed.

2. Teachers and other educators will achieve greater status in society as education is further recognized as basic to a strong economy, a sound defense, and a viable competitive position among the nations of the world. As schools are seen as the basic building block of society, teachers and other educators will receive salaries on a par with other professionals. Equity and parity will be addressed as basic to any merit pay system.

3. Teacher performance will be more closely supervised, and evaluation systems will become more effective.

4. Schools will offer more courses, including advanced information and skills, since many future jobs may not require a four-year college degree.

5. Schools will provide, or serve as sites, for the retraining and education of an increasing number of adults as many jobs become obsolete every five to ten years.

6. Businesses will provide schools with up-to-date equipment and assistance as they further realize that well-educated people are basic to their success.

7. Teacher certification standards will be monitored to allow only people

with specific knowledge and skills to teach in schools.

8. The proportion of minority students in the schools will increase dramatically. Schools will be expected to provide education and training to help these students become contributing members of society. Language skills, dropout concerns, teacher training, parent/citizen involvement, and high expectations will accompany this trend, and schools must deal effectively with each.

9. Educators will work to convince employers that students from urban/ inner city schools can perform as well as other students.

10. Teachers will develop, and schools will demand, better educational software that will enhance or replace textbooks.

11. Schools will become even more involved politically in making legislators and governors more knowledgeable about education.

12. Schools will seek alternative methods of financing which will increase the challenge of providing equal educational opportunity.

Impressive? Yes. Logical? Yes. Accurate? Maybe. It all depends on whether current educational leaders choose to be *causes* or *effects*—strategic planners or long-range planners—futurists or "pop" futurists. It may just be that there are systems of education yet to be created that will render the very language of these predictions obsolete.

The Case for Strategic Planning In Education

The recent groundswell of interest in planning among professional educators is a clear indication that strategic planning is an idea whose time has come in public education. Exactly why, it is difficult to say; other than it seems within the past several years many factors have combined to create major concerns at every level about the very nature and purpose of public education in this country. The Presidential Commission's report, *A Nation At Risk*; the Carnegie Commission's report; the National Governors' Association's *Time for Results*; several "education summits"; the negative impact of teacher strikes and fights over merit pay; the unsettled question about the accountability of educators and the achievement of students; declining tax bases; the continuing flight to private schools; charter schools and vouchers; teacher shortages; adverse federal policies that curtail funding; community splits over special interests; bureaucratic state departments of education; politically dominated local

5

boards; inept school administration; unaccountable "decentralizing" of education in the name of reform; a Congress that still believes the answer to effective education is preventing dropouts and raising test scores and punishing non-performing schools; and court orders that have nothing to do with education—all seem to have combined into a quiet crescendo of confusion and doubt even among the very best educational leaders.

The seriousness of that frustration needs no elaboration. It is no overstatement to say that the mere thought that public education has lost its way threatens the very existence of the nation. The Hebrew prophet Hosea said it best: "Without vision, the people perish." The simple fact is that a democratic society cannot exist without an effective system of universal public education: the first requirement for self-governance is an enlightened citizenry capable of governing themselves.

The Trauma of Change

But there is more. There are at least four other universal factors that further threaten public education. But these factors, inescapable as they are, overwhelming as they seem, carry within themselves possibly the only opportunity for the salvation of the American system of public education—if, that is, educational leaders choose now to create a future worthy of their heritage and equal to the nation's potential.

These factors taken together account for—and, in fact, constitute—the unprecedented change that has happened in every aspect of American life in the past few years. That traumatic change has forced concentration on the future because, suddenly, the future is now. Dr. Neal Berte, former President of Birmingham-Southern College, who himself is a true futurist (he initiated the "new college" concept), has suggested that now within the short span of two years, more change occurs in the way Americans live and do business than was wrought by the entire industrial revolution.

Paradoxically, this historic change was almost exclusively the direct result of modern education systems. Yet, at the same time, because of the profoundness of the change, most existing education systems were rendered, if not obsolete, at least seriously deficient in their ability to prepare students for the twenty-first century; or, perhaps more pertinent, in serving educationally all citizens under all circumstances in both the present and future.

These change factors have been well publicized by "pop" management and "pop" futurist writers; but most have ignored the present and, therefore, the future, implications for public education. Specifically, the changes most affecting public education—both as threat and opportunity—are (1) unprecedented demographic shifts and reformations; (2) the transitions of the nation's economy from agriculture to manufacturing to information to e-commerce, and now to bio-genetics; (3) the corresponding transitions in mainstream personal values, and (4) the intensification of global competition and the consequent redefinition of excellence.

The Need for Leaders

The conclusion of all this is simple. Whether these factors become curses or blessings will be determined by one thing and one thing only—local leaders. What is needed is not the type of phony leading that relies on the power of position, the political savvy of the boardroom, the doling out of favors, or the sleight-of-hand of inconsequential studies, surveys, and reports. But this leading must be the kind that is based on deep conviction and clarity of purpose; that courageously chooses from a variety of possibilities a definite course of action and concentrates all effort on specific purpose; that insists on measuring the achievement of those goals by present results; and that inspires others to follow.

In short, it's the kind of leading that plans strategically. After all, a leader is just someone who gets to the future before anyone else; and his or her greatness is measured by the time of his or her arrival and the number and kind of people who followed.

CHAPTER TWO

THE METAMORPHOSIS OF AMERICA'S SCHOOLS

There are four kinds of change irresistibly and traumatically affecting public education in America. In fact, taken together, these forces amount to crisis.

By now, these changes are not new. They have been touted and lamented in essay, conference, and video cassette since the early 1980s. And yet their implications are still not fully understood. What understanding there is, is mostly intellectual titillation without any emotional grasp of the urgency of the circumstances.

DEMOGRAPHICS

The first change is the unprecedented upheaval in the demographics of this country. While almost every commonly recognized demographic factor is involved, there are three that have primary significance for education: the aging of the population; the diversification of the family; and the transition from a nation with minorities to a nation of minorities.

The Aging Population

The first factor is the aging of the population. Facts acclaiming the "graying" of America are so familiar that they have become clichés. These are only a few examples:

- The median age is now 36.3
- 50 percent of the labor force is now over 40
- Every 10 years, the number of people over age 85 doubles
- There are 1 million people in this country over 100
- Two-thirds of school patrons are "empty-nesters"
- 32 million citizens are over 65 years old.

The first, and most popular, interpretation of these predictive trends is purely economic. And I suppose it should be. Almost every issue before Congress for the past three sessions has somehow involved the emerging conflicts among senior citizens, the aging "boomers," and the rising generation. One can better appreciate the poignancy of the tug-of-war when it is understood that in 1956 there were seventeen workers for each person on social security, compared with the present ratio of three to one, and the imminent ratio of two to one.

Adding an ironic dimension to this struggle is the fact that seventy percent of the wealth of this country is controlled by people over fifty-five. At least one demographer has noted the recent dramatic growth in a heretofore unheard of group, the "Sippies" (Senior Independent Pioneers); that is, those people who rode the inflationary spiral of the eighties and nineties to considerable wealth, cashed out their $30,000 houses for $300,000 or more, and moved to West Palm Beach.

When educators discuss the aging of the society, invariably the focus of their attention is the alleged decline of support for public education from "empty-nesters." The fact is that already seventy percent of the schools' constituencies are older people without children at home. Yet state and local funding for education in this country still exceeds by far that in any other nation—even Japan, where education is the national priority.

Perhaps that helps explain all the hue and cry in recent years for both excellence and accountability in our public schools. Much of that pressure is coming from people old enough to remember public education of an earlier time and mature enough to realize the consequences of anything less than the best. If their support is not immediately forthcoming, it may mean that they do not oppose public education, but instead are disappointed with what, in their perception, it has become. In fact, in at least three national surveys, citizens over fifty-five overwhelmingly judged education to be America's number one priority, and overwhelmingly indicated their willingness to bear the expense—but only if the education system satisfied their high expectations.

Beyond economic support, the aging population presents at least two significant windfalls for education. In the first instance, the fact that people are living longer means that most—both men and women—will enjoy not one but as many as three distinct careers over the course of their lifetime. It has been generally acknowledged for years that the average worker changes jobs seven times in a career, but now the prospect is for several completely different careers. Traditionally, it was supposed that public education existed to prepare a student for a single productive career, sometimes via higher education or technical or professional training. But now, one must prepare for progressive careers—the first through the traditional K-12 programs; the others through whatever might be evolved from nontraditional curricula or current adult and continuing education programs.

It is a moot point to argue whether public education exists to support a national agenda or to satisfy individual needs. The simple fact is that ultimately both will be served, and ultimately through public programs designed to prepare students of all ages for primary, secondary, and even tertiary careers. Of necessity, some education system of the future will have to position itself either to provide an early basic education that will equip students with the knowledge, motivation, and values to make those career transitions as they occur; and it will position itself for ready intervention at those critical life junctions.

One thing is clear, the aging of the population alone—as a single external factor—is enough to compel leaders in education to rethink everything about education: its governance, its curriculum, its funding, its delivery systems, and its purpose.

The Restructuring of the Family

The second great change factor posing both threats and opportunity for America's public schools is the reconfiguring of the family. This fact comes as no surprise, but most of the implications have yet to be realized. "Restructuring" is actually an understatement. In 1955, sixty percent of the families in this country consisted of a father, mother, and two children; today, that "typical" nuclear family of four amounts to only seven percent. In fact, the Internal Revenue Service recognizes at least thirteen variations of the family.

The basic problem facing education is that the present system was designed to accommodate the traditional family. Yet, there is a whole litany of facts and predictions about the family and family life that, taken together or separately, offer convincing evidence that public education is being forced to deal with a new world on its own terms. It is not that the adults in restructured families are lacking in love or concern for their children. It's simply that in many cases, the resources, support systems, and protective environments that were supposed to be a part of the "traditional" family are impossible to recapture. It is then that the rupture between the family and schools takes on many tragic proportions.

But all of the statistics are but cold recitations until they appear in the classroom in the form of substance abuse, emotional disturbances, behavior problems, health crises, and sexual irresponsibility—all to say nothing of the basic needs for nutrition and safety. For example, the mere fact, startling as it is, that there is no known cure for AIDS and that the nation is in an epidemic compels emergency attention for sex education starting as early as the elementary grades. And the emergence of the drug culture with the attendant violence demands at least an inquiry into basic values if not outright moral instruction. The question, as with all the other concerns, is who will provide the instruction or service.

Suddenly, the old phrase *in loco parentis* has gained real meaning. During the past two decades, every conceivable social and legal responsibility has been sloughed off on the schools; and educators, by their benevolent nature, continue to say "yes" to any and all demands placed upon them by other institutions in a state of deterioration and malaise. The result is that public education seems now so besotted with gratuitous functions, some conflicting, that it cannot clearly distinguish its primary mission, or so encumbered with the negligence of others that it cannot energize itself to make its own way. But like nothing else, the change in the family structure will demand a resolution from the schools.

Sooner or later, public education must either declare its magnanimous intent and omnipotent ability to serve as surrogate family, or begin to draw fine lines of distinction between possibility and impossibility, between what is the proper role of public schools and what is not. Such focusing may indeed be essential if public education is to achieve the concentration of effort and resources necessary to achieve excellence.

The Emergence of Minorities

The third major change factor with which public education must deal straightaway is the emergence of a diverse and, in many areas, dominant minority population. The United States is rapidly becoming a nation of minorities:

- One-third of all students currently in public schools are minorities,
- Over half the students in fifty-three American cities are from minority groups.

Quite obviously, there are too many implications of this development to discuss here, but three considerations seem to loom above all the others, especially from the standpoint of public education. The first is the very basic question of language. The whole business of educating (*educare*) presupposes communication; and communication presupposes a common medium. The issue has already produced all sorts of gyrations, quirks, and general craziness in local language curricula as well as legislative mandates.

In a more serious if not more responsible vein, already one-third of the States have moved to make English their official language, and momentum now seems to be sufficient to achieve national adoption. The primary motivational force behind such a move is more than majority dominance, Anglo pride, or mere convenience. It is the realization that a common language is the one essential bond of any nation, if that nation is to be identified by more than geographical boundaries: a common language is basic to any culture. Yet, at the same time, it is rapidly becoming a practical necessity for active professionals and others involved in daily business and commerce to be bilingual, even trilingual.

Second, there is the generally acknowledged but inevitable conflict of values, not the least of which is the challenge to the actual value of formal education itself in the life of the individual. What has for generations been held by mainstream America as the primary means for achieving the American dream has little meaning for those who for whatever reason do not or cannot share that dream. There is fundamental and unyielding resistance to an imposed discipline of learning whose only promise is that which is either irrelevant or unachievable, and whose consequences provide little immediate gratification. The implications of this conflict in values are broad indeed, ranging from the appalling dropout rates in schools and attendant delinquency and joblessness to the nation's long-term economic security, and even to the very question of a democracy being able to sustain itself through an "enlightened" citizenry.

The fact is that all American institutions—the Constitution, the Bill of Rights, the legislative and judicial branches of government, the education system, and all other aspects of the current established order—were predicated on a monocultural society. It will be interesting to see how long present systems can exist in a polyglot society.

Third, there is the emergence of the "mosaic" phenomenon which is simply the reverse of the old "melting pot" theory. In quite dramatic ways, amalgamation is being superseded by consolidation. Racial, ethnic, and cultural identities are being not only celebrated but cultivated with a combative assertion generally foreign to the American experience. It is a matter of pride arising from the distinction of uniqueness within a diversity that obscures value systems. That is to say, it is the simple necessity of identity. It is also a matter of the security found in the familiar within a diversity that is sometimes unmanageable.

All this means that public education faces a future in which there is bound to be a dramatic shift in the delicate balance that exists between the values and interests of the various groups and those more readily identified with the broader society, with the advantage being held by the groups.

The first question thus posed to public education is threefold: whether it will be adaptive or creative in the transition; or will it flounder in optimistic futility waiting for things to settle; or will it actually provide stability through bold leaders committed to a visionary kind of national synergy (or, as someone once said: *e pluribus unum*).

The second question regards the validity of localized educational programs as opposed to national mandates and agendas. Sooner or later the diversification of America is going to force education to come down on one side or the other. Simply stated, the necessity to address local concerns and student needs must be weighed against national mandates that in attempting to deal with the needs of all achieve little for anyone. It would be considerably more ennobling if that decision were made out of concern for the individual student and implemented with community courage.

But, the most serious social problem facing the nation's schools, if not the nation itself, is: How can the education system accentuate the richness of cultural diversity while at the same time honoring and preserving traditional American values? It is rather sobering to watch the passionate, inexorable unification of Europe—a unity that far transcends the mere economic motives of the European Common Market. It is frightening to have witnessed the complete and final deterioration of the Soviet Union along ethnic, racial, and cultural divisions. It would indeed be a tragic paradox of history if, say in 2010, there existed the United States of Europe and the United States of America, like the Soviet Union, had become balkanized.

Redefining "Public" Education

It is manifestly evident that these three unprecedented demographic phenomena alone—aging, family structure, and minority population—are enough to demand unprecedented radical changes in America's system of public education. Mere superficial changes in the way schools conduct their business are pathetic, verging on tragic; what is required is a fundamental change in the nature of the business itself.

ECONOMIC TRANSITIONS

The second great change that predictably has become both the impetus and substance of strategic planning is the unprecedented transition in the economic base of the United States, if not the world. This change, although at first gradual and always progressive, even predictable during the past 150 years or so, in the late 1970s began to compound itself in both its implications and its velocity, resulting in continuing economic instability and confusion and, in some instances, outright desperation. The effects have been felt alike by governments, corporations, families, schools, and individuals.

In the early '80s, the book Megatrends introduced Americans to something called the "age of information" and generalized the historical transitions in the economy of America. The fundamental concepts are both accurate and intriguing; but the most significant issues involved in these transitions are yet to be fully realized, even by historians—to say nothing of futurists.

The basic approach holds that "ages" or "eras" are characterized in terms of what the majority of the nation's population does to make a living. So, the thesis goes, as late as the middle nineteenth century, about seventy percent of Americans were involved in agriculture as their primary source of income. The "agricultural" or "agrarian" age historically extends all the way back to pre-civilization, even to the beginning of the human race. That means, as a conservative estimate, that the "agricultural age" is about 25,000 years old. In 2000, less than 1.5 percent of Americans made a living farming; and that percentage continues to decline.

The shift from agriculture came with the industrial revolution of the

15

nineteenth century. It is not generally noted, but in America, the movement into and through the "industrial age" came over a period of at least ninety years—from 1860 to 1950—and occurred in three approximately thirty-year increments. The first was that of private industrialization, characterized by the entrepreneurial industrialists of the middle and late 1800s. The second was that of corporate industrialization, characterized by corporate enterprise—as opposed to purely free enterprise. Corporate industrialization ran its course with the stock market crash of 1929, and, with the consequent intrusion of government aided and abetted by both the national war effort in the late thirties and early forties and the increasingly liberal social philosophy of the nation, was transformed into a social institution. The third was government industrialization which manifested itself in the "military-industrial complex" as well as in a complicated economic interrelationship between the federal government and all corporations. The last great surge of government industrialization came in the frantic rush into outer space in the ten years immediately following the Sputnik surprise in 1957, and the economic interrelationship between government was further tangled by civil rights and other social issues ranging from worker safety to redistribution of wealth.

It was not until the late seventies that the nation realized that yet another economic transition had occurred, taking the government, industry, and everybody else quite by surprise. According to the popular notion of the time, as proclaimed in a variety of pop-futuristic publications, the nation, if not the world, had suddenly been thrust into the "age of information." The experts knew that because, by their count, sixty-five to seventy percent of the population was making a living in so-called "information" industries.

Actually, the "age of information," an apt description for the time, did not break out as suddenly as most observers seem to think. The transition from the "industrial age" to the "age of information" occurred over a period of at least thirty years, and in identifiable increments of roughly ten years each. The first—from the late fifties until the mid-to-late sixties—is best described as The Discovery of Ideas; the second—from the late sixties through the mid-seventies—was a time in which The Awareness of Ideas was the nation's chief attraction and, in some cases, distraction. It was not until the late seventies that The Assimilation of Ideas manifested itself in attempts at forming networks and linkages to connect all the accumulated and erstwhile relatively

16

independent ideas into usable communities of information. That is when America discovered "the age of information."

In many ways America's discovery of the age of information was quite fortunate, if not inevitable, because other factors of the seventies combined to pose an insurmountable threat to industrialism: the first great oil "shortage," emerging second and third world markets and dramatic increases in industrial production in these countries, and governmental machinations in world economies. So, the much heralded "information and service age" might not have been so much a real advance in the economic scheme of things, but the only available alternative at the moment. Unfortunately, the alternative now seems to have been limited by both time and substance. The plight of the laid-off steelworker—an artisan who drove a cab until he could return to work at the mill—is a fitting metaphor for the predicament of an entire nation.

The ancient Greeks had a persona for just about everything imaginable. Their unfortunate, chauvinistic idea of "opportunity" was a nude female figure wearing woolen boots and completely bald save for a single lock of hair growing tuft-like just over her forehead (hence the expression, "seize the opportunity by the forelock"). Opportunity not thus seized becomes a tragedy of loss, and so it was with the rapid, unprecedented shift of the economy. The first shock was felt in local and industrial economies. The national unemployment rate soared to almost twelve percent, and entire communities, built around single industries, were devastated. Even ten years later, the national unemployment rate still hovered around six percent (almost twice that of the industrial age); and in some areas such as Allegheny County, Pennsylvania, entire communities still were ravaged by upwards of fifty-percent unemployment. If not typical, at least indicative of the profound subsidence in the economic base of the nation is one mining town in West Virginia which as late as 1990 still was suffering from 95 percent unemployment.

All the classical economists since Adam Smith have insisted that there are only three sources of wealth: agriculture, mining, and manufacturing (sometimes fishing is added as a fourth category, but usually it is subsumed under agriculture). Any other human enterprise merely shifts around the wealth, variously represented from time to time by something called money. The problem is that shifting money, while it accumulates more money at the point of shifting, sadly does not create wealth. Debtor nations like the U.S. would do

17

well to remember that; and those people, businesses, and nations who stake their economic security on enterprises in information and services will eventually discover that their economy and their security depend on wealth producers. Emphasis on wealth-producing activities is especially critical in a period of massive resettlement of the earth's economic plates.

Beyond Economic Transitions

Far transcending the more historical process of these basic economic transitions, and ultimately more significant than the substance of the transitions themselves, are the implications thereof, implications that are as pervasive as they are radical. Almost all of these will directly affect public education, but there are at least three major issues that, together or alone, will forever change every aspect of education — its structure, content, delivery, even its basic purpose. These are (1) the question of knowledge/information manageability; (2) the inevitable emergence of an information/knowledge-based caste order; and (3) the trauma of total-system obsolescence.

The Management of Information

First, information/knowledge management. The great knowledge explosion of this century, because of its hyper-popularization through management seminars and television commercials, has become generally acknowledged as one of the conundrums of the age—so generally acknowledged, in fact, that acknowledgment has turned to acceptance, and acceptance to ambivalence. Unfortunately, in this case, ambivalence is tantamount to catastrophe. Nuclear energy comes immediately to mind.

Any extensive recantation of the enormity of this issue would fail in the attempt. So, ironically, it might best be understood in terms of a simple paradigm that, admittedly, is more anecdote than argument. Originating in the synthetic sixties, it held rather starkly that the universal body of human knowledge had doubled in ever-diminishing intervals, as follows:

From 4 B.C. to A.D. 1900,

From 1900 to 1950,

From 1950 to 1960, and

From 1960 to 1965.

From 1965 to 1990, it doubled every three years.

From 1990 to 2000, it doubled every 18 months.

Now, its rate is incalculable.

One of the yet unexplained mysteries of the age is that even in view of this astounding accumulation of knowledge, Encyclopaedia Britannica, during the 1960s, was determined to get it all between the covers of something called a "syntopticon," sold, of course, by subscription—proof positive that human knowledge is exceeded only by human folly.   Now all that knowledge ostensibly is on the internet. And, syntopticons and their like have lately given way to palm pilots, wrist-sized computers, dvd players, and digital cameras—revised, moment by moment.

It is not surprising that the modern technocrats—who, by marvelously omniscient machines, collect, collate, sort, and otherwise "process" this knowledge and information in all its various forms toward ultimate information gridlock—still do not really understand the meaning of "information management." Intent as they are either on making and selling "hardware" and "software" or on personally self-actualizing as a career "computer expert," all their systems and applications are but a superficial, albeit profitable and convenient, feint at management of information. The basic problem is that, so far, computers and the internet have been used to formalize, perhaps even fossilize, traditional thinking processes, not to engender new ones. Furthermore, productivity analysts for the first time began in 1999 suggesting that technology has actually reached the point of diminishing returns — except in the computer industry.

What a chance missed! With the advent of the computer, for the first time in history the human mind was freed from the drudgery of menial intellectual exercise; but rather than seizing the opportunity to explore the vast and indescribable capacities of the mind, the entire race gleefully set about deifying predictability and conformity in thinking by something called "state-of-the-art." It is doubly ironic that even the so-called "critical thinking" taught by most schools is programmed. The mere programming thwarts real thinking; simply responding to options is not always thinking. Furthermore, critical thinking is essentially a matter of judgment, and judgment is essentially a matter of values. Programmed values are anti-thought. The phrase itself is a classic oxymoron. Nevertheless it is still encouraging to know that schools of the 1990s were at least recognizing the possibility of expanding human

19

capacity through any form of so-called "higher order thinking". However, effective and progressive education of the future will concentrate not on critical thinking skills, but on values-based creative thinking. That dimension of the human intellect is a force very possibly without limit. That kind of creativity is generally shied away from because it cannot be managed at all in traditional ways. And the mere mention of the higher psychic powers of the mind is heresy among the computer orthodoxy and the traditionalists in education.

Sooner or later, however, someone is going to realize that the most critical issue of the early twenty-first century is not war and peace, nor famine, nor the environment, nor poverty, nor anything the world troubles itself with now. The one critical issue is discovering the ultimate function and power of the human mind: that discovery will prove to be the historical equivalent of the discovery of fire. The only thing that can forestall or prevent that discovery is education.

The Polarizing of Society

The second implication of the shifting concern of the nation is the evolution of a new caste system within the American, perhaps global, society based strictly on "knowing." Knowledge— the great equalizer—quickly becomes the great denominator, separating the society into classes distinguishable not by birth or rank, but by intellectual acumen. While the various classes and, therefore, the lines between them may be imprecise or obscure, the extremes of the continuum are alarmingly visible and grow farther apart with every new discovery or new idea. Already, the terms "elite" and "underclass" have been accepted with poignant new meaning into the vernacular. The fact that half the population of the United States are illiterate is often quoted, but always without understanding or remorse.

Professional and academic degrees—M.D., M.B.A., J.D., and Ph.D.—are the peerage of the American social order. This elitism is vaguely reminiscent of the intelligensia of eighteenth and nineteenth century Europe and, even more remarkable, of the Greek Gnosticism of the first and second century. The result is a broad range of contemporary and future social, political, and economic consequences.

For example, the primary social issue deriving from the circumstances involves the single most fundamental ingredient of society itself—that is, a core of common values. No social unit—family, community, corporation, tribe, state, or nation—no matter the size, can exist without the bonding provided by a common value system. A culture is simply a collection of values. Values and value systems are of two kinds: those that derive from conviction (religion, superstition, codes of honor, et cetera) and those that derive from need (a la Abraham Maslow). In most societies, these two kinds of values interact to produce practical rules of personal behavior and individual responsibility. Sometimes the rules of that interaction are referred to as "ethics." Quite obviously, a community dichotomized by ignorance and knowledge will not share the same convictions, nor will it collectively perceive the same needs; and, therefore, it cannot identify either its cultural benchmarks or its ethical reference points. Ignorance and knowledge cannot produce the same values. And such basic conflict within a society can only erode its moral synergy and lead ultimately to the deterioration of that society.

The primary political issue deriving from this circumstance strikes at the heart of a democratic form of government. Plato observed that a democracy would fail only when its citizens discovered that they could vote for themselves anything they wanted. Democracy presupposes an "enlightened citizenry"— people who are, in fact, knowledgeable and prudent and disciplined. There is a fine line between a democracy and anarchy. And laws are a fragile thing. America seems lately—during the past three decades—to have invented a malevolent hybrid in a kind of "politicized anarchy" in which special interests override laws and governmental procedures. Special interest groups thrive on the manipulation of both the populace and political systems through misinformation and disinformation—more specifically, by making and controlling knowledge.

This situation, of course, is based on the assumption that all segments of the society have full participation in the political process, as they supposedly have in present-day America. But without that, there is a danger even greater than self-destruction. The simple fact is that, ultimately, those citizens who lack the knowledge necessary to participate effectively in self-governance run the risk of being disenfranchised, *de facto*, if not *de jure*. After all, knowledge is still power. And, in either case, there emerges a ruling class—the elite, the cognoscenti. Suppression, if not oppression, of the service classes is a natural

21

consequence.

The conclusion of the matter is this: A democracy cannot exist without effective public education—an education system that ameliorates the extremes, that also reconciles all those differences within society that are irreconcilable without a common base and level of knowledge.

Finally, the fundamental economic issue deriving from this circumstance is the question of individual economic status: whether economic dependency or economic self-sufficiency. Unlike earlier times, in the modern world, gnosis and intelligence translate almost invariably into material well-being; and as the extremes of knowledge grow farther apart, the wealth of nations is posited evermore toward the knowledge end of the spectrum. The resulting severe trauma is realized in at least three ways.

First, and most obvious, is the wide variance in the quality of life that can be experienced at the extremes. While in one case luxury becomes a necessity, in the other merely satisfying necessity is a luxury. This simple conflict has been the precipitant of most Western revolutions, tomes of political theory, and the crux of liberal economic ideology of the twentieth century. Yet, despite the enduring, incalculable effort to politically redistribute wealth, poverty and affluence are constantly redefining each other. The fact is that there are no political solutions to economic problems. It is almost a paradox: The economic balances of any society drive its politics; but, ultimately, politics—especially in a democracy—cannot drive its economic balances. It seems the laws of wealth are not subject to the laws of men. Suddenly, economic and political reality, as well as basic reality, demands that any consideration of the value of anything be superseded by the affirmation of the value of life—all life.

Second, there is the simple yet explosive matter of economic rule. The old quip that "he who has the gold, rules" is more fact than facetious. Somehow, one suspects, that is true even in a democratic society whose majority is fully enfranchised and politically active, although uneducated and impoverished. To be more specific, there can be no political freedom without economic self-sufficiency. In twenty-first century America, this implicit conflict far transcends the age-old struggle between master and slave, lord and serf, owner and employee. At issue here is the tense relationship between democracy and capitalism and whether that unique American symbiosis can be sustained. The answer depends on only one thing: that is, the degree to which that socioeconomic relationship allows for individual self-sufficiency (and the attending self-direction)—not as a patronizing entitlement—but as a result of discretionary individual effort justly rewarded.

Third, and intensely human, there is the matter of individual life-control; that is, the ability to effectively manage one's own life. While it is true that personal happiness does not derive directly from economic advantage, it is clear that economic disadvantage most often severely restricts higher aspirations and dramatically curtails individual achievement. As the economic chasm widens, the society is thus inevitably separated into two groups: those who live with hope and those who live in despair. With hope, because they have the privilege of choice; in despair, because they have no apparent options. With hope, because they can exercise reasonable control over their own destiny; in despair, because they depend strictly on luck, fate, chance, and magic. That such widespread abject hopelessness could occur in a society that has recognized, even extolled, education as the one great source of hope is not as much an indictment of education as of that society itself—and its hope.

System Obsolescence

The third implication of the shifting economic base of the nation is the simple and profound principle of obsolescence compounded to total-system-breaking proportions. It is as simple as paper being replaced by screens, parchment being replaced by paper, papyrus being replaced by parchment, bark and tables of stone being replaced by papyrus—all variations of systematized symbolic human communication. It is as profound as communication in both inner and outer space through energy impulses—totally different in kind, a non-symbolic system.

The now commonplace accelerated obsolescence of jobs within computer industries is but a dramatic synecdoche of the industries themselves, because there is a principle at work here larger than any system. In fact, it is a principle inherent within all systems, processes, products, organizations—anything that has been or can be created. It is the irresistible principle of "life-cycle," the inevitable curve of progression/degression between birth and death. Configured and given numerical dimension, it might appear like this:

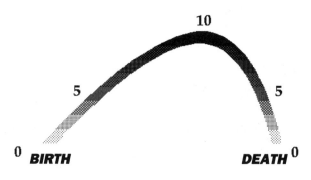

The subject is born at "0" and, continuing the metaphor, proceeds through infancy, childhood, adolescence—maturing at "10." At that point, it reaches, according to the Greeks, "crisis"—by definition, the point at which the entity either lives or dies. There are no other options. Stability, homeostasis, even continued equilibrium are out of the question. One of two things will happen: First, the "10" may become a new "0" and initiate a whole new life-cycle; or, second, the "10" simply declines to "0." Post-crisis might be depicted like this:

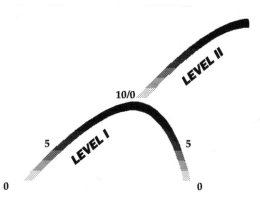

Crisis is the point of separation between those who lead and those who manage. In fact, the first test of leading is the ability to apprehend crisis.

The secret to survival is the recognition of a crisis before it occurs. If crisis passes unacknowledged, recovery is improbable. Recognition, surprisingly enough, is a rather simple matter: The sole indicator of crisis in any entity is parity between investment and outcome—the break-even point. The sole

24

indication of obsolescence in a mature entity is unfavorable disparity between investment and outcome; that is, when it costs more to sustain the system (however cost is defined) than the system can produce (however production is defined).

Perhaps the best current example of this phenomenon (railroads being the classic example) is electrical utilities. Having developed over the years, at great cost, both a system and a mentality for the delivery of electricity, they find it compulsory to transform all kinds of energy—solar, nuclear, thermal, magnetic, wind—into electricity, simply because that is the only kind of energy the system is capable of delivering. It has not occurred to them—or they have not admitted—that human beings already possess the technology for site-based power generation—energy derived directly from the source. That is why nuclear energy in the hands of electrical utilities will always be an economic disaster. Refinements and improvements of the existing electricity delivery system only compound the deficit.

That public education in America is at crisis has been declared by every credible witness. Whether crisis has passed remains a debatable question. The *Presidential Commission's Report (A Nation At Risk)*, studies by the Carnegie Foundation as recent as 1998, the National Science Foundation, the National Governor's Conference, as well as feature editorials in *Forbes, U.S. News & World Report,* and *Newsweek,* and best-sellers such as *The Closing of the American Mind and Cultural Literacy,* and a barrage of declamatory statements by business leaders and politicians all testify that there is something urgently and irreparably wrong with the nation's system of public education. Yet none provide real solutions.

That which is past is past. No one can argue against or disparage the unexcelled accomplishments of public education in this country. It alone is the vehicle—the force—that has brought Americans to the highest standard of living ever achieved by any nation, any time. And it has been the means by which untold millions of citizens have achieved personal freedom, dignity, and fulfillment. But that which is past is past.

What is needed—in fact, what must occur—is not a revolution: That would discount and demean all the former triumphs of public education. It is not an evolution: That would require the perpetuation of a system already obsolete. What is needed, rather, is a metamorphosis—a total change of form, which

25

presupposes a total change of substance. *Morphe* is absolutely the right word in this context—not *schema*. And therein lies the fundamental difference between this change and the changes of the past. Almost without exception, changes in public education—even those hailed as avant garde, modern, or innovative—have, sadly enough, been merely *schematic*, and for that reason superficial. They wrought little or no change of substance. They were merely schemes—variations within a system.

The plethora of so-called "reform" movements, loudly heralded by the federal government, governors and state legislatures, are for the most part simple-minded, politically expedient impositions of change-retardant schemes upon school systems whose obsolescence is guaranteed with every passing law. And, students, as well as national interests, are suffering irredeemable loss. "continuous improvement," "schools of choice," "site-based management," "vouchers," "restructuring" have become cruel clichés, and "empowerment," an impotent one-word oxymoron being used to grasp authority without accountability. None of these will work because none of them can work. Even more disastrous, these terms and concepts only serve to reinforce existing traditional systems. There are two, albeit inextricable, aspects of this unforgivable confusion: (1) the question of leading or direction, along with attendant accountability, and (2) the nature of the fundamental issues themselves.

Regarding the first, simply stated, no one—from the White House to the classroom any longer knows for sure who is in charge or who is accountable for anything. And if they did, the intractable governance and management systems in place would not allow for either right action or performance accountability. Most local administrators serve so many masters that they, at best, can manage only ambiguity and tentativeness. And teachers have heard so many uncertain trumpets that many have abandoned the field in despair.

Regarding the second aspect of confusion, the reformation of education in America has been a travesty of tragic proportions. All so-called "reform" legislation, which purports to define the terms of the reformation, has paradoxically reinforced the traditional—the status quo. By insisting on prescribing in authoritarian (and sometimes whimsical) fashion standardized curricula, uniform teaching methods, artificial performance evaluation schemes, rigid minimum competencies for all students, and bland sameness in the guise of equality, legislators essentially have rendered impossible any real reformation. Reformation has been reduced to increasing test scores, and decreasing dropout rates. Either no one can see or will acknowledge the fact that the real task of reformation is the radical transformation—a *new* creation—of every facet of the American education system—its purpose and scope, its governance, its teaching and learning dynamics, its curricula (if there is such), its time and place—all with a new dedication to developing the original genius in the mind of every student. This means a complete change of all education paradigms, of definitions, of disciplines, of vocabularies—perhaps of values. And that is the purpopes of strategic planning.

One final word: If a system does not continue to create itself, parallel systems grow up alongside and replace it. The rise of these new systems is gradual, but the collapse of the old is sudden and unforgiving.

THE TRANSFORMATION OF MAINSTREAM VALUES

The third irresistible change affecting American education is the dramatic transformation in individual human values, especially those mainstream values that have emerged since the mid-1980s. That actual mainstream personal values do exist and can be identified is attested to quite pragmatically—sometimes crassly—by national advertising. But value systems are not static. In quite broad historical terms, American mainstream personal values have paralleled the nation's economic transitions and, in fact, have been precipitated by, if not derived from, the necessary and fundamental dynamics of each successive economic era. That is to say, each economic period of the nation's history was and is accompanied by a corresponding mentality, a mentality that reflects the essential dynamic of the economic system. That mentality in every case encompasses, among other things, a certain world view, a certain view of human life, its worth and purpose; a certain view of self and others; a certain concept of roles and functions within a society; a certain philosophy of government; and, not surprisingly, a certain economic ideology.

The recent turn in mainstream values looms especially significant, not just because of its immediacy, but because it probably represents a radical departure from—or a reaction to—the previous somewhat evolutionary transformations in personal value systems. If so, this is a change of incalculable proportions. The best evidence that it is a radical departure is the abject failure of corporate and educational organizations to recognize it and adjust to it, and their consequent current demise from unknown causes.

The Cambridge Group has accumulated over the past fifteen years convincing evidence regarding the nature of these value shifts. But perhaps the simplest way to get at this complex phenomenon is to begin with an abbreviated version of a matrix analysis first offered by Carolyn Corbin in *Strategies 2000*. This provides insight not only to the progressive nature of the value changes; but also suggests a wide range of interrelationships, causes, and effects.

Economic Era	Primary Resource	Transforming Agent	Time Orientation (Values)
Agrarian	Land	Natural Energy	Past
Industrial	Capital	Processed Energy	Present
Information	Mind	Knowledge	Future

This chart obviously requires no elaboration, except the column describing the shifts in time orientation. First, there must be acknowledged the basic premise that time orientation is indeed the fundamental expression of a value system embracing a total self/world view. Second, there must be an understanding of the relationship between that view and the economic dynamic it parallels. Only then will the values themselves be recognized as the primary driving force behind every other aspect of a person's life; the force sustaining or otherwise confounding corporate exigencies; and, ultimately at a national level, the force behind every major social and political imperative.

Agrarian Values

The agrarian values were and are predicated on the belief that the past is sacred, because the past is the only route to the future. That is, the past is always prologue—the foundation of and the impetus to that which is future. It defines and invents improvement, progress, achievement. That kind of perspective gives a special kind of meaning to all present activity and effort as it inevitably turns into the past. That explains why agrarians were and are the last optimists, believing that by dint of their own effort today they can create something better tomorrow. And, it is as simple and as fundamental as the dynamic at the heart of the agrarian economic system: plant today; reap tomorrow.

Over and over, in surveys and interview sessions throughout the nation, those persons with an agrarian mentality, when asked to draw a single line that represents either their lives or human history, draw an inclined plane. That is their basic view of both themselves and the world. And it is an interesting thought, and perhaps somewhat sobering, that it was precisely that value system that was responsible for, among other historic accomplishments, the American system of public education.

By disposition and by desire, agrarians are "builders." And if now they often look to the past in pleas to "return to basics" or even in more radical demands for reform, it is only because, to their great disappointment, the present has not kept faith with the past.

The Values of the Industrial Age

The industrialite mentality is characterized by a monomyopic emphasis on the present—completely void of any notion of either past or future. And this view also derives from the dynamic of the economic system, quite different from the agrarian dynamic. The vocabulary says it all: If the primary resource is capital (no longer land), then engaging that resource with a transforming agent (not labor but automation and monetarization) becomes an investment (not planting) for the purpose of generating a return (not a harvest). And soon the industrialist learns that the increments of return on investment, since they do not depend on natural cycles, can be shortened by spurring consumption of goods, products, and services.

So the economic dynamic proceeds in stages: (1) the making and selling of goods, products, and services that either are in themselves expendable, or are designed with calculated built-in life expectancies (therefore, the most inspiring word of this dynamic: "new"); (2) the convincing of an otherwise reasonably content but potentially insatiable public that the *summum bonum* is getting and spending (therefore the most sacred religion of this dynamic: "materialism"); (3) the creation of competitive consumption through power advertising that guarantees satisfaction (therefore, the most preferred philosophy of this dynamic: "the one who dies with the most toys wins"); and (4) through raising the very basic activity of foraging to the status of "professional shopping" (therefore, the greatest discovery of the dynamic: "I can get it for you wholesale").

This dynamic is relentless and never-ending. Labor is transformed into purchasing power, and there is never enough. Work becomes a means, not an end. And there is always too much.

That is the reason people with an industrialite mentality draw their lines and human history as a straight, flat line—dull, boring, redundant, tedious, without purpose, without joy—the very image of the assembly lines and the bureaucratic institutions through which they accumulated an uncontrollable consumer debt. It is ironic that consumers ultimately consume themselves.

The Values of the Age of Information

The mainstream values of the information age represent a convergence of three fundamental experiences inherent in the dynamic of the economy of this era: (1) systems thinking; (2) obsolescence; and (3) globalization. First, the very basic enterprise of this age was the "systematizing" of data or information— "interfacing," "networking," "linking"—all terms ultimately conveying a sense of connection far beyond that simply of "mainframes." It was not so much an altruistic Donnesian notion of the interdependence of humanity as it was an overwhelming realization that not only is personal well-being inexorably linked to systems surrounding the individual, but also that all human existence does in fact depend upon an indeterminable number of delicate connections in a complex infrastructure called civilization or, more precisely, American civilization.

That system was shattered by the Arab oil embargo of the seventies and the deep recession of the early eighties. The people of the affective "we" generation quickly developed high anxiety when they discovered the acute tentativeness in the ganglia of economic, political, and social connections upon which their lives depended. Unaccustomed to such fragility, they raged about to establish and strengthen systems deemed adequate to guarantee the perpetuation of their world: IRA's and Keoghs, Medicare, estate planning; Reaganomics and the Moral Majority; the family, fraternity and the country club—all desperate attempts to forestall the disconcerting confusion that occurs when the unfamiliar meets the uncontrollable, when the center can no longer hold, and things fall apart. For the first time in their history, Americans experienced the pall of ambiguity.

30

Second, beyond the obvious practical obsolescence deriving from the eruptive shift in the economic base during this time, there was a more subtle and greatly foreboding certainty of obsolescence in the systems themselves, systems which became outdated even before they were put in place. Paradoxically, the inexhaustible profusion of systems negated the permanence and, therefore, the security heretofore implicit in all systems. Always before, systems had been the primary means of imposing order. Authors as different as Nathaniel Hawthorne and Thomas Carlyle constantly ruminate on the blessings and curses of the "systems" by which all people order their lives.

But with the information age, all order was subject to constant reordering, rendering all order disorder. Rigid organization was transformed into mere *Postmodernism* shifting patterns of innumerable designs; long-fixed reference points were permanently obscured by infinite variations of scanning; and the definition of reality changed impassionately with every extrapolation. The stark recognition of mutability was quickly transmogrified into a strange tripartite fascination with heraldry and genealogy (the comfort of the past); aerobics and Rolexes (the assertion of the present); predictions and corresponding remedies of all kinds (fear of the future). For the first time in their history, Americans experienced the quiet hysteria of permanent impermanence. The future became a matter of doubt.

Third, exacerbating the twin loss of order and permanence, was the growing awareness of globalization. No system of information can be complete, it seems, until it is linked with the entire universe. The unabated extension of systems brought the world together with the touch of a single key, but it also produced, in the same instant, a cacophony of urgent imperatives regarding the universal human condition. Famine, pestilence, disease, war, poverty, greed, brutality—all in their vilest and most inhumane form—were visited daily, through elaborate quick-response global information systems, upon the hearts and minds of people who, in their erstwhile isolation, had considered such degradations, if at all, beyond the pale of their existence.

America's first response was, as it always had been, a response of conscience mixed with condescension: to put things right all around, according to their own standards, and by intervention financially, militarily, politically. But then Americans, to their chagrin, suddenly discovered three astounding realities: (1) the world's insatiable and increasingly vociferous demand for goods, products, and services required to achieve Western standards at most and survival at least; (2) the surprising levelling that had occurred among the wealth of the industrialized nations with the restructuring of the global economy; and (3) the advent of international competition, for which America was ill-prepared, in both productivity and trade.

Suddenly, the great patron of the world—because of its own deficits, weakened currency, and volatile stock market; because of its own impotent and confused military blundering here and there throughout the world; and because of its own political disarray deriving from a moribund hypocrisy in the White House to a rancorous petulance in the Congress—found itself in the unlikely position of not only being unable to direct the affairs of the world, but—God forbid—even unable to look after its own well-being. Soon it became evident that all the elaborate security "systems" that they had constructed were not, and could never be, adequate to guarantee their future, as they had known it.

So, in an acceptance born of anxiety, Americans passively began to acknowledge that their standard of living could not be preserved for subsequent generations, and that even their own earlier aspirations had become unattainable. Goal setting gave way to lottery tickets; and achievement became mere survival. And for the first time in their history, Americans began to see the future as less. It is no wonder that the information-age mentality depicts human history, and life itself, as a declining plane; and sees human beings not as builders, or even consumers, but as restive dependents.

The Values of the New Age

Within the past five years, yet another economic system has evolved, and with it—perhaps in advance of it—a new predominant mainstream value that correspondingly reflects the dynamic of this economy. If the chart is extended to accommodate the New Age, it appears like this:

Economic Era	Primary Resource	Transforming Agent	Time Orientation (Values)
Agrarian	Land	Natural Energy	Past
Industrial	Capital	Processed Energy	Present
Information	Mind	Knowledge	Future
Biogenetics	Life	Morality (or legislation)	Being

On a rather dull Saturday morning in May 1987, most major newspapers carried the same front page photograph and accompanying story. Actually, the story was not new; it had been brewing for over two years. But, suddenly, it had come to court. It was about a genetic engineering firm in the Napa Valley that had invented and patented a new form of bacteria that, if sprayed on strawberries growing in the field, would render the fruit frost-proof—ergo, its name "ice minus." The only difficulty was that there was some bothersome evidence that those berries, thus treated, would kill people. Some people tried to stop the spraying. The courts had to decide. This simple case and this simple choice are at once both the harbinger and the epitome of the New Age.

First, there is the fact of biogenetics or genetic engineering as practical commercial enterprise. No longer is the alteration of life forms a subject confined to experimental laboratories, Orwellian novels, and horror movies. It has been elevated to the very highest level of professional scientific inquiry and achievement and, at the same time, gained a somewhat blase acceptance from a public that only recently would have considered such tamperings "unnatural." Moreover, it has become the basis of an entirely new economy—perhaps even wealth producing.

It is worth noting, particularly in light of the recent depression in the nation's farm economy, that biogenetics is most directly tied to agricultural products—both crops and livestock. Paradoxically, agriculture is (and will likely continue to be) the primary economy in which biogenetics realizes its greatest commercial success.

It is only when biogenetics is posited toward the human end of the life continuum that morality becomes an issue. At present, there are in the U.S. Patent Office over 4,000 applications for bioengineered life forms; only two dozen or so propose to produce radically altered creatures. But already, members of the Society for the Prevention of Cruelty to Animals are becoming concerned about the ethical issues of reinventing life. The prospect of genetically engineering people has cast the question of ethics or morality into an entirely new context. In addition, a whole host of related moral issues arises. For example, one of the most disturbing issues still facing the Congress and the Courts is the question as to whether it is "ethical" to utilize the body of a woman as a manufacturing plant to produce fetuses to be used in the treatment of Parkinson's disease. The only reason such barbarism is legal today is because of a Presidential executive order issued in 1993. And the prevailing political thinking is to allow it. When morality fails, laws are the last resort. When laws fail, executive orders are the first resort.

The advent of this new age, and the discovery that human beings now have both the capacity and the inclination to recreate themselves in their own images and according to their own imaginations, evidently has also led to a new discovery of life itself. Specifically, it has demanded a redefinition of the human "being." Because if that being is a matter of any number of options, as indeed it appears to be, then what shall be the proper substance of that *being*? Its purpose? Its function? And by what standards will it be judged successful? Or is that an appropriate question? It is more than metaphorical that people of the new mentality view their lives as a circle, not cyclical, but compassing. Perhaps there is something here originating in the Kierkegaardian existentialism of an earlier age; but now it has emerged as an uncompromising pragmatism characterized by an individualism approaching selfishness. It is not the expansive, rugged individualism of the pioneer; but the focused, protective determinism of the settler.

The best and latest primary research indicates that the new being recognizes eight life components. (A life component is defined as any aspect of a person's life in which he or she can set goals.) Using the circle symbolically, the components are as follows:

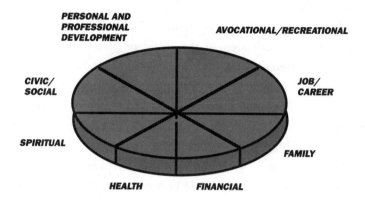

These components require little explanation, but the change in mainstream personal values regarding them needs to be understood.

- **Job/Career:** The dominating life component of the one-dimensional industrialite. The industrialite's primary identity (as in, "What do you do?"); and first obligation (as in, "work for a living"). Now, one of many life components, blended into or subordinated to the others. Personal identity is likely to transform the job; the workplace must accommodate the worker; work itself must be made a source of satisfaction or pleasure; and loyalty to any employer is not expected.

- **Family:** Once a private sequestered world, a necessary refuge when there was no other place to go. Customarily sacrificed to ambition, achievement, and corporate demands. Something to be controlled. Now, a delight; a source of celebration; itself an achievement; a commitment that transcends not only the job, but all other life components. The highest priority.

- **Financial:** Once, the anxious security of a regular check, the promise of a retirement program; or the quick accumulation of wealth; the very reason for any enterprise. Now, the interaction of various economic activity into the totality of one's life adequate to achieve a continuing total self-sufficiency. Good fortune is sought and accounted in the present tense. The primary reason collective bargaining is on the decline; individual bargaining is on the rise.

- **Health:** Once expendable, an expected loss; an excuse for malingering; a reason for commiseration. Now, itself a precious gift, worthy of preservation; the energy source for all human endeavors; the most valuable possession a

35

person can have.

- **Spiritual:** Once confined only to that which was thought to be religious and other-worldly; forbidden in the world of practicality and reality; a relationship between someone and God or something. Now, a realization of the pneumapsychosomatic nature of every person; the practical reality of the human spirit when manifested in self-esteem, motivation, aesthetic appreciation, manners, and respect, as well as reverence; the *a priori* and ultimate relationship between people.

- **Civic/Social:** Once mostly a matter either of compulsion or convenience; a ploy of special interests; a crusade or a retreat for the idealist. Now, an expression of interdependence, of kinship; an honest commitment to the service of others; an urgency to preserve and strengthen the community against the menacing onslaught of poverty, crime, ignorance, and war.

- **Personal and Professional Development:** Once of no consequence in a world characterized by both complacency and hopelessness; futile before the circumstances of luck, fate, chance, and magic; survival as only justification. Now, the vitality of hope, the essence of vision; the only means of creating and realizing opportunity; excellence as a final reward.

- **Avocational/Recreational:** Once only a diversion, an escape; an elixir; a sedative; a filler for leisure time. Now a studied pursuit of personal awareness, an expansion of self; a nurturing and regeneration of one's humanity; the continuing emergence of one's self.

The mainstream personal values of the new age obviously do not derive simply from the existence or nature of these life components; but, rather, from the relationship they each and all bear to and among each other. *Syzygy* is close; *synergy* is closer, but not spot on. *Sophrosyne* is most accurate: that is, "balance," "self-control"—or more precisely, "harmony"—and that is the ultimate meaning of "being."

All this may seem, upon initial consideration, somewhat theoretical; but it is as real and as practical as any office, assembly line, work station, kitchen, or classroom. The implications for systems of education are twofold: First, there is the overwhelming impact on organizational and operational considerations; second, there is the decisive effect on the very purpose of education. And there's serious challenge to the current notions about both.

The values inherent in "being" put all traditional organizations at risk,

36

especially corporate enterprise. This is the one fundamental reason giant American corporations are, and have been, irreversibly declining—not because of the strength of world competition, but because of disease within. It is common knowledge that the business world is plagued by inefficiencies, loss of productivity, greed, strikes, shoddy workmanship, hateful service, and general irresponsibility and carelessness. Studies have for several years indicated that most Americans do not like their jobs. It is revealing that almost all employees rank job satisfaction or meaningful and challenging work as what they want most from their job.

The more enlightened companies try desperately to keep their organizations functioning—quarter by quarter—at a modicum of profitability. Employee motivational programs, quality circles, classes on possibility thinking, identifying corporate cultures, emphasis on quality of the workplace, decentralization, reading books about reinventing the corporation, and a plethora of affective, qualitative remedies have been frantic but vain attempts to satisfy either the companies' purposes or the need for individual being.

Sooner or later, that need for being will be served. That is why the most critical issue facing any organization—corporate, political, religious, educational—is the alignment of individual interests with the interests of the organization. Unfortunately, it seems that ultimately there is an irreconcilable conflict between the necessities of the traditional organization and the well-being of the person.

The assertion of individual being over the exigencies of the organization certainly is a major contributing factor to the phenomenal increase in the number of entrepreneurial small businesses. In fact, eighty percent of the growth in the nation's economy in recent years has come from companies with fewer than one hundred employees. Organizations of this size, are by their very nature more closely attuned to the individuals who comprise them. There is more likely to be a mutual interdependence and, thus, a more mutual benefit.

Educational organizations have not been immune from the stagnation and disruption resulting from the conflict between personal interests and those of the organization. Tolerance of mediocrity in the name of tenure, negotiation impasse and strikes, early retirements, the mass exodus of some of the best teachers, low self-esteem among professionals, institutional inertia, and low student achievement are all dramatic indications of a general mood of personal dissatisfaction among educators.

Most school districts have recognized the seriousness of the situation and many have, to their credit, attempted to deal with approaches similar to those prevalent in business. Administrators have embraced—sometimes naively, usually prematurely—a variety of fixes: participative management, site-based management, teacher empowerment, teaming, quality circles, and anything else that has the aura of savvy business measures.

However, as with corporate enterprise, there will be no permanent resolution of the conflict between individual being and the necessities of the organization until the organization is completely reformed, with at least as much emphasis on the total well-being of the person as on the person's production. Ironically, that is the only way to achieve production.

The second impact of the values implicit in being is on the very basic purpose of education. While there is no stated purpose of education in the United States, historically, school has been the means by which people were prepared to make a living by working in a corporate enterprise. In recent years, even legal and health professionals, to say nothing of artists, have found themselves part of a corporated system.

But with the decline of corporate enterprise and the inversely corresponding growth of free enterprise, the purpose of all education must be seriously reconsidered. Interestingly, American education has, in recent years, moved in the right direction, if for the wrong reasons. Emphasis on the whole person, higher thinking, values, and character are all precursors of a new curriculum that develops individual being. The fact is that personal independence, moral integrity, individual responsibility, achievement, invention, genius, compassion, confidence, and self-respect may already be as basic to the successful human being as reading, writing, and arithmetic.

Truly educated people of the next century will not apply for a job. And they will not be slaves of a corporation designed to expect them to produce stockholder wealth. They will create their own enterprises—not as a way of making a living, but as a vital part of a whole life.

COMPETITION

The fourth great change affecting public education is unprecedented competition in the free market, worldwide. It has come as an amazing discovery here at the beginning of the twenty-first century that the axiomatic motto of modern economics is at once its clarion, its theme, and its epitaph. The notion of supply and demand generally held as orthodoxy for over 200 years is exactly backward. Especially in a world bound essentially by a single economic system, the more accurate formula is demand and supply. The fact is, demand has always created supply.

The Digital Age, with its instant and universal access to the world of everyone else, has raised the expectations of the rest of the world to Western standards—specifically, American standards. The "Globalization of Tastes" has long been recognized by astute marketers; and the recent forays of Coca-Cola, Levis, Revlon, and other American staples into the likes of China and Russia is in happy response to a demand that even governments cannot deny.

In fact, there is in the world today more demand for goods, free markets, products, and services than ever before. And, as political freedom and wealth are shared by more and more people in former Communist and so-called developing nations, the demand can only increase. In fact, there seems to be no limit.

Correspondingly, never has there been more of a supply of goods, products, and services. The worldwide availability of capital (the world is awash with money), entrepreneurial ambition (the profit motive is a genetic trait of homo sapiens), and management talent (MBA's seem to outnumber people) have, for the time being at least, in almost all areas of demand created an oversupply, and that is precisely the circumstance of competition.

Public education has been forced by circumstance into competition. The unparalleled demand for education—especially that which is excellent—has made education the biggest business in the United States, possibly the world. And where there is opportunity, free enterprise will most assuredly and quickly be found.

It is not generally acknowledged by educators, but public education has already entered the free market, simply because free enterprise has entered the business of education. But it may not be until public education is completely privatized that school administrators will discover that the competition is not the friendly private or parochial school, although new private schools are opening at a rate of one each day. But the real competitive threat is from for-profit corporations that are expert in capturing selected markets, extremely skillful in developing curricula and educational programs responsive to market demand, comfortable with performance guarantees, and unhampered by maudlin altruism about social responsibility.

The question for public education is simple: How can it compete in the free market? The answer is also simple: innovation, technology, and excellence.

First, innovation. Sadly enough, public education is not known for its creativity or courage; but rather for inertia, homeostasis, and convenience. Except for the wild frenzy of experimentations that broke out in the 1960s which fitfully ran their course and then died from exhaustion, America's schooling has changed very little since the Industrial Revolution. The very fact that schooling can be used and understood in this context is all too indicative of the system's resistance to change and its resolve to serve primarily the personal convenience of those involved in it. In fact, the first concern in the operation and administration of public education seems to be the convenience of staff, parents, students, and the community at large.

Peter Drucker admonished long ago that it is not enough to do something right; the important thing is to do the right thing. It is a sad commentary on the leaders of public education—and, indeed, precipitative of the current crises in the nation's education—that all of its evaluation systems, methods, instruments, and techniques are devoted toward measuring how well something is being done (and that usually by subjective appraisals of processes). Very little effort has been made to determine whether the thing in question should be done at all. It is a pitiful condition to be found doing the wrong thing right. Or as one official of a now-defunct manufacturing company recently mused, "We were working like hell up to the day they closed the doors."

The second answer to competition is the full application of state-of-the-art technology. Educators seem generally loathe to admit it, but the internet has rendered time and space moot in teaching and learning processes. The concept of going to school, as in building and classroom, is as obsolete as the timeworn industrialite debate over pupil-teacher ratios. There is no question that the teacher will always be the primary catalyst in disciplined learning, but the role of the teacher is being totally redefined by factors other than technology. In fact, it may be that education itself is being totally redefined as well. Technology has created limitless opportunities for learning—both in terms of the amount of information and knowledge that exists and the accessibility of that information and knowledge. Since learning is a natural human activity, occurring often accidentally, coincidentally and randomly, perhaps education must be properly defined as any learning with both intent and discipline. And that kind of education can occur anytime, anyplace. That plays havoc with traditional so-called delivery systems.

The third and most conclusive answer to competition is excellence. There is an old axiom well known in the retail business that holds, "In good times, everybody survives; in hard times, only the best survive." That is to say, the final test of long-term marketability of any good, product, or service is its high quality. As competition intensifies, the higher the quality, the greater the likelihood of surviving and surpassing; the lower the quality, the greater the vulnerability. It seems that people will always buy the highest quality— sometimes even when they cannot afford it.

It is most interesting that, for at least the last decade, a great deal of verbiage regarding quality and excellence in education has been loosely thrown about by both critics and professional educators—most of it in the form of placebos to appease dissatisfied customers who are adamantly refusing to accept anything less than the best in America's schools.

Unfortunately, educators have seemed loathe to define excellence in education, presumably because such a definition would incur corresponding accountability. It is remarkable, and somewhat of an indictment of professional educators, that every other profession, trade, craft, job, skill, hobby, or any other human enterprise has established definite, recognizable indicators of excellence. Yet education languishes in the smug vagueness of indefinable variables and political considerations. But sooner or later, public education will realize what business has known for a long time: Ultimately, all quality is defined by the consumer. That is especially true of excellence.

The greatest obstacle facing professional educators as they attempt to define excellence in specific dimensions and by certain standards is the general predisposition to be "everything to everybody." And that notion is exactly contrary to the very nature of excellence. Excellence is nothing less than strength compounded. It results only from concentration of effort—not from dissipation of effort. The broader the focus, the less the likelihood of high quality. Real excellence can be achieved only within a context of a narrow, specifically defined purpose.

41

A case in point. Recently a manufacturing-sales company found itself in serious difficulty with regard to profitability. A wise business counselor turned the company around with just three questions to top management. The first question: "How many products does your company make and sell?" No one knew. That was the first clue. When the product line was counted, management was surprised to discover that the company made and inventoried 146 products. Why, they did not know. Second question: "How many products is the company actually selling?" No one knew. Supposed all. Second clue. A thorough analysis of sales, resulted in a traumatic revelation that ninety percent of the company sales was in twenty-six products. Third question: "Of these twenty-six products, how many actually produce a profit?" No one knew. But by now, a new state of awareness had been reached.

When a thorough analysis of profitability—item by item—had been completed, the company realized that ninety-five percent of all its operating profit was being derived from only eight related products. That company now has eighty percent of the world market in those products; and they can charge virtually any price because consumers will always pay for the best. The customers who buy from other sources are those who are willing to sacrifice quality to cost.

The ultimate test of character for any person or organization is the point at which known excellence is compromised.

In business, such specialization is referred to as "niche marketing." The specialty is the market niche. It is worth noting, in this discussion of competition, that true evolutionists postulate that the way the species survived was not by "survival of the fittest" as commonly interpreted. The popular myth is that the strongest survived mortal combat with competing species. However, real evolutionists know the species survived, not by killing each other off, but by finding a niche—a special, limited place where they could not only survive, but also prosper. In that sense, they were fit for—or fitted to—their environment or marketplace. And, indeed, the fittest survived—and still do.

The "niche" principle is as applicable to education as it is for the species and business. It is certain; it is absolute. The problem, obviously, is determining in a chaotic environment, sometimes self-induced, just what the proper niche of public education must be if it is to survive and prosper. Like most other truths, the answer is quite simple, but the translation into reality is difficult and it requires both great vision and great courage.

The simple answer is localization—intense and unremitting localization. Excellence cannot be realized through measures set by federal and state mandates. Excellence cannot be normed. The mad rush in America to standardize education ironically has had, and will continue to have, a deleterious effect on the quality of education. Excellence cannot be standardized, homogenized, or predetermined for school systems across the nation. Excellence, rather, must be discovered and defined at each and every locality—even down to the building and unit level.

That is not to say that national norms and standards are not useful. They are; but not as goals. National norms should be considered merely reference points by which the local system is able to judge its performance in a universal context. Invariably, the standards of excellence established by visionary, courageous school districts always exceed those prescribed by external authorities.

Somewhere in one of his poems, Robert Frost describes the predicament of being caught between twin millstones. This is an apt analogy for the dilemma that education has forced upon itself. And the dilemma has no resolution given the current constraints of education in America. On the one hand, there is the hue and cry for excellence, albeit erroneously interpreted by test scores; on the other hand, the demand for democracy, meaning "same."

As long as education in this country is conceptualized and realized in terms of a single continuum—a continuum in which the two ends continually judge each other, allowing for comparison, rank, and value differentiation—then there is really very little hope for excellence in education for everyone. Excellence will be achieved by learners outside the system rather than within it.

The Urgency for Change

These four kinds of change: demographics; economic transitions; the transformation of mainstream values; and competition are inexorable and irresistible. If they are to be managed, they must be met with leaders—a new kind of personal leader characterized by bold vision and unrelenting commitment.

43

CHAPTER THREE

TOWARD A DEFINITION OF STRATEGIC PLANNING

The Different Kinds of Planning

Just as sure as strategic planning is an idea whose time has come for education, there is a distressing overabundance of ideas about what strategic planning really is. Almost overnight, it seems, a bevy of planning experts has arisen with a confusing array of "models," formats, and processes for "strategic planning." After all, consulting is the second oldest profession. The result is that planning quite often (1) produces nothing but disappointment; (2) becomes a series of costly false starts; (3) leads to the complete abandonment of formal planning; or (4) becomes a facade hiding reality.

For that reason, strategic planning should be understood first as distinctive from other kinds of organizational planning. The distinctiveness of each kind of planning derives from both methodology and context.

For example, **comprehensive planning** may be undertaken by any size unit with authority limited to improving existing aspects of the organization. Each component is identified and assessed in terms of performance, needs, or future projections or even expectations. But planning is restricted to what already exists. Such are most accreditation self-studies — pre-configured, preconformed to "standards," all assumed to be exclusive, essential, and permanent. This kind of planning usually perpetuates institutions through static systems and meaningless jargon.

Long-range planning, likewise, may be done by any size unit with limited authority to be both selective with regard to the components considered and original in terms of response. This kind of planning seeks out "intersections" between the current state of business and the world, either as it is or is projected to become, and then prescribes adjustments to that reality. Aspects of the organization's current operations or, perhaps, even new initiatives, become the focus of the plans. By practice, if not by philosophy, long-range planning does not provide an overriding context in which to measure the efficacy or interconnectability of the disparate plans; but rather develops each more or less in isolation, pursuing its own reconciliation of what *is* with what *will be*. The assumption is that there is a natural congruence with the aspects of the organization not selected for future emphasis. However, there is no actual validation of the other existing components of the organization which were not selected for planning. Typically, this is the kind of planning used for curriculum, staff development, facilities, communications, or any other single component of an educational system.

Program planning is the process of creating a grand design to make a concept operational. This kind of planning is usually conducted within the context of a larger organization and, in fact, is typically assigned by, or derived from, the initiatives of that larger organization. Exploratory by its very nature, program planning becomes a kind of evolutionary process. Its purpose, quite simply, is to take a single idea, test it against reality, justify it by intended outcomes, and describe how to make it work. In the end, the emphasis is on sustaining functions, relationships, and results.

Usually this kind of planning follows a predictable, although somewhat flexible, pattern: identification of the subject, sometimes in the form of a hypothesis; assessment or evaluation of need; analysis of information regarding the current status of the subject and surrounding conditions; verification of the need for the program; establishment of goals and objectives for the program; an extensive, detailed design of functional relationships, accountabilities, and outcomes; a description of the system to be set in place for monitoring and controlling the program; and, finally, specific standards and methods of evaluation toward improving or refining the program.

In a school_district, this kind of planning is that usually employed in developing plans for public relations activity, counseling, extra-curricular activities, community involvement, and the like—anything that lends itself to being systematized or programmed.

Project planning , as the term implies, is the logical, sequential process of advance designing any significant task to accomplish a specific purpose. The next stop is implementation. Typically, the initial steps used in this process are those of rational decision-making:

(1) Identification of the task

(2) Analysis of status and/or situation

(3) Establishing the project's objective

(4) Identification of alternative (possible) courses of action

(5) Analysis of the obstacles and adverse consequences related to each possible course of action

(6) Decision regarding the basic course of action to be taken.

When the basic course of action is decided, then detailed plans for necessary management activities can be developed, such as: basic strategies, sequences, and timing; organization; allocation of resources; staffing; directing and controlling; evaluation; and, if appropriate, provisions for recycling the project. The project planning process is used to accomplish initiatives such as building construction, campaigns of all kinds, and any other stand-alone activity.

The Context of Strategic Planning

Strategic planning is the means by which community continuously creates artifactual systems toward extraordinary purpose. Implicit in this definition is the concentration of all efforts, resources, activities, and energies toward a single goal. The Greek word for a military general was *strategos*; that is, one who leads (*agein*) and army (*stratos*). The *strategema* were the daring, yet prudently calculated, plans by which the leader concentrated efforts on controlling circumstances and events, thereby ultimately achieving triumph.

The significance of all this is that strategic planning is not defined by methodology, process, or system; but by the context in which the plan is derived. Quite simply stated: *Only strategic organizations can do strategic planning.* Plans developed by non-strategic organizations or units, even though the planning schema resembles that of strategic planning, can be at best comprehensive or long-range.

To clarify this issue, there are four, perhaps five, distinct characteristics of a strategic organization or unit. First, a strategic organization is **autonomous** ; that is to say, it is self-governing. Quite obviously, no organization is absolutely autonomous: All are subject to laws, regulations, and the like. But when an organization is a legal entity, that status both grants and requires self-governance, usually in the form of a board of directors. Non-strategic units, on

47

the other hand, exercise either delegated or functional control, which means, essentially, that they are governed.

Second, strategic organizations have the prerogative and the responsibility to determine their own identity and to actualize that **identity** by performance. Non-strategic units have identity and purpose only within a strategic context and their performance is based on factors over which they do not exercise final control.

Third, strategic organizations have the prerogative and the responsibility for the acquisition and allocation of **resources** of all kinds. Non-strategic units request and manage resources allocated to them.

Fourth, strategic organizations are responsible for creating and nurturing their own **culture**—the values and vision that lead, guide, and sustain everyone who is a part of that organization. Non-strategic units are charged with the responsibility of realizing the vision, upholding the values, and emulating the leader of the strategic organization.

Fifth, as a practical matter, strategic organizations develop plans that are expansive in both **range** and **scope**. The range may be five years and beyond; the scope entails the entire system.

The conclusion is abundantly clear: Strategic planning must always precede non-strategic (or sub-strategic) planning. Organizations who do otherwise soon discover the real sting in Einstein's memorable phrase: "The perfection of means; the confusion of goals."

What Strategic Planning is Not

Having narrowed the definition of strategic planning to the means by which a smaller unit concentrates all its efforts and resources on constant recreation to achieve extraordinary purpose, there is still a necessity, given the current vogue of planning, strategic and otherwise, to understand what strategic planning is *not*. Unfortunately, there are many false prophets in the world proclaiming a gospel of hocus-pocus flim-flam. There are eight popular misconceptions.

Planning: Not a Model

First, strategic planning is not a "model." That word—and probably, even more, the concept—makes a very dynamic process nothing more than a dull, uninspiring scheme that can be superimposed on any existing organization or circumstance. This approach to planning becomes nothing more than a filling in of the squares on a crossword puzzle, painting by the numbers, or connecting the dots. Many school districts, believing a model to be a means of making planning either easier or "right," have discovered too late that the only result "models" achieve is the model itself.

Planning: Not Just a Process

Second, strategic planning is not an endless intellective frenzy to be reveled in *ad infinitum* by a host of celebrants raptured by process and disdainful—if not fearful—of results. The school district that attempts to plan by creating a full and fancy bureaucratic planning department staffed by a host of research and statistic experts; foundering for years in the collection of trivial information, the development of theory, and the postponement of decisions; and by involving hordes of uninformed, uninterested, and unexcitable so-called "publics" will ultimately find that the best way not to plan is to plan. To wit: One school district—admittedly of considerable size—embarked some time ago upon a course to the future with a crew of eight "professional" planners; a passenger list made up of several thousand people from various publics arranged into fifty or so committees; a cargo of inconsequential minutiae brought together from all kinds of wonderfully strange places; all on a three-year odyssey of mystifying business. At last report, they were lost at sea.

Planning: Not an Academic Exercise

Third, strategic planning is not an academic exercise. Its end is not to explain, not to analyze, not to hypothesize, and certainly not to demonstrate an author's ability to cut and paste facts and speculations into highfalutin tendentious conclusions. In short, strategic planning is not thesis material. Neither is strategic planning an extended exercise in problem identification bereft of solutions. This approach is that of the confirmed amateur planner who confuses planning with confusion.

Typically, this is the approach pandered about by so-called "centers" for this, that, and the other—usually having something to do with "research." Typically, the only product they provide is a dazzling collection of megatrends and millidata arranged so as to be untranslatable into any kind of action, to say

49

nothing of sense. Unfortunately, many very professionally run school districts and corporations have learned from these "planners" much more than they ever wanted to know about expensive futility.

Planning: Not a Prescription

Fourth, strategic planning is not a prescription. One of the, if not *the*, saddest ideas about strategic planning is that it is very much like a physician's prescribing a remedy for a patient who is, or who is about to be, sick. Except in this case the physician is a "consultant"—an expert who has a wide variety of remedies all mixed up according to patented formulas, and who dispenses them to the infirm for a substantial fee, plus expenses.

This is the kind of planning usually done by high-powered firms prestigiously located in North American centers of sweetness and light. It is this kind of planning that has been severely criticized by distinguished business magazines, like *Forbes*, for being little more than grand bunko schemes. In fact, one business magazine recently referred to this kind of planning as the "seagull" approach: "The consultants fly out of Boston, circle around the client a few times, drop a strategy on them, and fly home."

Usually, such firms have one or two really good professional planners. But these one or two professionals are even more dedicated capitalists, so the client is seldom given the benefit of their experience and skill. Most of the client's actual planning activity is directed by a recent MBA graduate who has no experience, and only textbook knowledge.

The major drawbacks to prescription planning, other than the exorbitant expense, are four: (1) The recommendations of the prescribed plan are quite often irrelevant (done somewhere else by someone else); (2) they are usually impractical (read once in a book), and (3) implementation seldom occurs (not my job). Furthermore, (4) this approach all but prohibits local participation in developing the plan and, therefore, precludes local acceptance of the plan.

This kind of planning seems to be designed for those organizations that can afford more than they need because most such planning efforts are exorbitantly priced initially and subject to "add-ons" which, as it turns out, are always necessary to "complete" the plan.

Planning: Not an Edict

Fifth, strategic planning is not a edict. That is, it is not an autocratic pronouncement which is put together, often secretly, by those at the top of an organization and then passed down to be implemented by those at the bottom. But, unfortunately, this has been a rather typical approach to planning among education administrators. In fact, many superintendents are hired on the premise that they themselves will bring a new "program" to the district. And it is not uncommon for superintendents of long tenure to be expected by the board of education and the staff single-handedly to provide the annual operational plan.

No one can argue that anyone who is distinguished enough to be considered for a superintendency will not bring to the job and the district very valuable knowledge, philosophies, and skills. But, on the other hand, one cannot deny the oft-observed phenomenon that any change, after all, temporarily produces positive results. And no one can argue that veteran administrators do not have a treasure trove of experience and wisdom. But, then, no one can deny that single-handedness breeds single-mindedness; and that twenty years of experience may be just one year of experience twenty times.

Quite obviously, there are two major disadvantages of top-down, autocratic planning. In the first place, this kind of planning is always lacking in substance. The fact is, a plan's scope cannot exceed the capacity or the aspirations of those who develop it. The substance of a plan diminishes in direct proportion to the number of people involved in the development of it; when the number of participants reaches one, the "plan" becomes nothing more than a personal decree. The second disadvantage is a corollary to the first: As the number of participants diminishes, so does the very critical general support for the plan; when the number reaches one, the "plan" becomes no more than a lonely argument.

Edict plans are probably the most potentially dangerous of all the pseudo-plans because they can easily become a self-deceptive assertion of progress in the midst of regression.

Planning: Not Political Manipulation

Sixth, strategic planning is not political manipulation—not by the superintendent, not by the board, not by the teacher union or any other special interest group within the school system or the community. It cannot be profaned by creation of so-called "community partnerships" as a disguise for negotiation. Planning cannot be predicated on hidden scenarios and ulterior motives. It is not an occasion for bargaining or power plays. It is not a time for competition. And above all, it is not a machination of attitudes and wills toward a foregone conclusion. Planning is simply not planning if the conclusion is known in advance. If planning does not surprise, it will only disappoint. And for that reason, the degree to which a plan shocks is the real measure of its success.

Planning: Not a Budget

Seventh, strategic planning is not a budget. Budgeting is, after all, nothing but a nip-and-tuck process by which the pieces of a financial garment are made to fit. Of course, those who attempt to plan in this fashion are wont to make the claim that their budget reflects the organization's priorities. And, in reality, it does: It provides clear evidence that a budget has priority over real needs.

A "plan" that starts with an existing budget as a base completely ignores the possibilities and detail of the future; and even so-called "zero-based" budgeting (in which each and every expenditure is justified each year) places more emphasis on figures than on needs. Quite obviously, public institutions labor under financial limitations and restraints; but there have been very few good ideas that ever went lacking for funding—if the commitment was there. The simple truth is that strategic planning does not mean planning a budget; it means budgeting the plan.

Planning: Not a Substitute

Finally, strategic planning is not a substitute for leaders. If the organization has no leaders before planning begins, it will have none when the planning ends.

The Strategic Planning Methodology

Strategic planning ultimately must be understood for what it is, rather than what it is not. For example, not a "model," the strategic planning methodology is an effective combination of both a *process* and *discipline* which, if faithfully adhered to, produces a plan characterized by originality, vision, and realism.

52

The discipline includes the vital components of the plan itself; the process is the organizational dynamic through which the vital components are derived. Both the discipline and the process are aimed at *the means by which a community continuously creates artifactual systems to achieve extraordinary purpose*.

Strategic planning is not an endless intellectual frenzy—which is a substitute for decisions; but it is a voluntary commitment to generate rational decisions about the deployment of resources toward fixed goals and aspirations. The whole purpose of planning is to make decisions about the future before the future either forces the decisions or renders any decisions irrelevant; and to create action, not activity.

Strategic planning is not an academic exercise in theory analyses and problem identification, but it is an obligation to achieve measurable results, translated ultimately into performance by those individuals responsible for implementing the plan. The essence of a strategic plan is the identification of specific desired results, to which all the effort and activity of the organization will be dedicated. And the success of any plan is determined only by the results it produces.

Strategic planning is not a prescription from an outside expert, but rather a proscription that is formulated by the combined expertise within the organization. The fact is that the people who work in an organization know more about the organization—its problems, concerns, and potential—than any number of planning consultants could possibly know. Beyond that, the local people are just as aware of global issues and circumstances, and are even more particularly sensitive to the impact of those factors on their unique situations. And, certainly, they alone understand all the complexities of local issues. In any school district, the best planning consultants available anywhere are quite often the existing staff. They, together with the patrons, community leaders, and students already possess all the answers to the district's future. All they need are direction and impetus.

Strategic planning is not an edict, but a consensus plan derived through the application of the basic principles of participative decision-making; specifically, (1) the person doing the job is the expert; (2) that which is strategic must be validated by the operational; that which is operational must have strategic context to have meaning; (3) accountability, authority, and information are commensurate, and proceed in that order; and (4) decisions are made at the point of action.

In practice, these principles mean that, with reference to the organizational design, the strategic plan is developed reciprocally from both the strategic and the operational. Without this duality, the result is a plan that is either too broad or too narrow to gain a common commitment to goals and aspirations. A plan that is not based on consensus is not a plan; it is an altercation.

Strategic planning is not political manipulation, but an open, unrestricted examination of issues and earnest consideration by people of good will from each and every constituency of the district. The successful planning process can never be democratic; it must emphasize common interests rather than special interests; and it must seek mutual agreement rather than majority.

Strategic planning is not in any way whatever a mere budget whose only purpose is always to impose and frustrate creativity and confound excellence — in short, to limit progress. Strategic planning, if properly done, unleashes creativity from throughout the organization, sparks new enthusiasm for excellence, and guarantees progress without the artificial limitations of budgets—all because planning begins and ends with ideas and aspirations, not numbers. Budget planners can make the numbers work, all right; but strategic planners work the future.

The methodology of strategic planning consists of both a *discipline* and a *process*; the *discipline* describing the substantive ingredients or components of the plan itself; the *process*, the method or procedure by which the plan is created. To argue the relative value of either is moot; to attempt completely to separate them is foolish. Both are inextricably connected and, if properly interwoven, will provide a superior plan.

The *discipline*, if properly applied, will render the *process* entirely meaningful because it forces a complete and final resolution of all relevant issues. The *process*, if properly followed, assures substance in the discipline because it provides a controlled concentration of rational effort on the issues involved.

Definitions

The first step in any attempt at a planning method is the definition of terms. At present, that is somewhat difficult because terms related to planning—particularly the discipline—are helplessly bandied about with no regard for meaning and with little evidence of clear thinking. In fact, some planning vocabularies seem to be a kind of doublespeak devised to confound decision making and defy implementation. As with most other matters of the mind, the literal words themselves are not as important as the concepts they represent; but it is for sure that sloppiness in word use is a direct result of sloppiness in thinking. Therefore, the planning discipline must have a vocabulary that manifests and demands sharp thinking and that can be translated into precise, purposeful action. Reliable studies show that most so-called strategic plans fail because no one can prove for sure what the verbiage really means, if anything. For the record, that is the famous "kerygmatic fallacy"—the more you peel away, the less there is, until there is nothing at all.

Experience demonstrates that the most effective planning vocabulary is made up of fairly common, garden variety words given specialized meaning for planning. The simplest, most workable vocabulary for the planning discipline consists of about a dozen utilitarian terms: *Beliefs, Mission, Parameters (Policies), Internal Analysis, External Analysis, Objectives, Strategies,* and *Action Plans.* Also useful are the terms*Weaknessess, Strengths, Organization Analysis, Competition,* and *Environment.*

When these few terms, defined by the specific context of strategic planning, are arranged in a logical, progressive order, they provide the simplest, yet the most effective strategic planning discipline for anything, anywhere, anytime, by anybody.

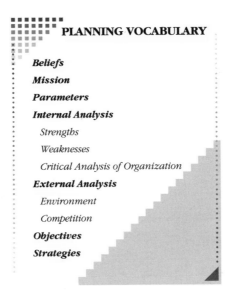

PLANNING VOCABULARY

Beliefs

Mission

Parameters

Internal Analysis

   Strengths

   Weaknesses

   Critical Analysis of Organization

External Analysis

   Environment

   Competition

Objectives

Strategies

CHAPTER FOUR

THE PLANNING DISCIPLINE

Beliefs

The statement of beliefs is the most logical, if not the most necessary, beginning of any strategic plan. It is a formal expression of the organization's fundamental values: its ethical code, its overriding convictions, its inviolate moral commitments. Essentially, it describes the character of the organization. That means that the statement of beliefs of an organization must represent a composite, a distillation, of the personal values of those who have a vested interest in the organization. In a school district, the belief statement reflects the common core values of the entire community.

The fact is that every organization has a distinctive value system, even though it may not be formally articulated, perhaps not even admitted. However, the statement of beliefs should not be merely an acknowledgment of what the organization is, but an expression of what it is at its best. Beliefs are, in fact, moral imperatives.

The statement of beliefs serves a dual purpose: First, it will provide the value system upon which the subsequent portions of the plan will be developed and evaluated; second, it will, as part of the published plan, become a public declaration of the organization's heart and soul. Because it is so important, the statement of beliefs must be precise in language and absolute in application. Long, rambling, hazy, philosophical treatises are neither precise nor practical and, therefore, have no place in a serious plan. These exercises in pompous futility are either pitiful attempts at saying something, or very pretentious ways of saying nothing.

Quite in contrast, an effective statement of beliefs is simply formatted, crisply stated, and easily understood. A typical statement by a school district may read like this:

We believe that:

- Nothing is ever accomplished without risk.
- All people have infinite worth.
- Excellence is always worth the cost.
- All people can learn anything.
- The first priority of any society is education.
- Every person has a right to succeed by his or her own definition.
- Thinking is of greater value than knowledge alone.
- The higher the expectation, the greater the achievement.

For further clarification, beliefs are not mere bland platitudes *sans* real value judgment ("People are essential"). They do not require validation by the real world ("All people have the right to personal freedom"). They are not prescriptions ("Everyone should be allowed to succeed"). They are not education specific ("Latin is best taught beginning in the third grade"). Rather, they are declarations of universal human values as held by the people who make up the organization; values they would hold no matter where they were, or under what conditions they found themselves, or what business they were conducting.

Mission

The mission statement is a clear and concise expression of the district's *identity, purpose* and *means*. Always written in one sentence, the statement should reflect both the clarity of thinking and the vision characteristic of leaders. While the mission statement must obviously acknowledge reality, it must also aspire to the ideal. Furthermore, the mission statement should not be merely a description of the *status quo*, but rather a bold declaration of what the organization will be. In that sense, it creates a new reality.

Above all else, the mission statement must represent a commitment to the special distinctiveness, the uniqueness, the oneness-of-a-kindness, the originality, that sets the organization apart from others like it. If an organization cannot identify its uniqueness, it probably cannot justify its existence. That means that all the options available to the organization must be seriously deliberated and a single identity agreed upon. Quite often school districts have the mistaken notion that their mission is so rigidly set by law that they have no choice at the local level. But most districts find, upon close examination, that in actuality, they have considerable flexibility and very few limits. In fact, the trouble usually comes in limiting the district activities.

The mission statement, like beliefs, serves two purposes—one in the planning process, the other in the application of the plan. In the first place, the mission is the keystone upon which the entire plan depends. Everything else in the plan springs from it and must be judged by it. But everything else also judges it. Because until all the remaining portions of the plan come together to prove the efficacy of the mission statement, it is at best tentative. In short, the mission tests the plan; the plan tests the mission.

The second purpose of the mission statement is obvious: In application, in practice, it serves to focus all the organization's attention and to concentrate all its energies on one common purpose. The mission is the one thing that should be known and eventually understood by every person in the organization; otherwise, how can anyone make any sense out of his or her job or other activities? There is simply no way to measure or describe the enormous positive impact that the knowledge of the mission by all employees can and will have on an organization. In other words, it is amazing what happens when everyone knows what he or she is doing.

On the other hand, lack of awareness can only result in cross purposes, fragmentation, and loss of productivity. Recently, a business experiencing financial and production problems hired a consultant to analyze the situation. Twenty-five of the top managers were asked by the consultant to write down the organization's mission. The tabulated result included seventeen different ideas about the basic purpose and function of the company. Little wonder it was in serious trouble. And, although the performance of a company and a school district will assuredly be measured in different terms, trouble is trouble in any language.

The mission statement of a school district must address the specific, local situation; and, therefore, it cannot be borrowed from others in the same business. Nor can it be just another academic foray into the wonderfully warm and fuzzy world of theoretical perambulations.

For example, no one so far has been able to say for sure what the following actual mission statement means, much less what action it mandates, and the only thing that could result from it is a warm glow. The best analysis of it is: meaning everything, it means nothing.

The mission of the Warmglow School district is to provide a quality educational process designed to enhance the student's life-long ability to experience his or her maximum potential in an ever-changing world and to work for the betterment of mankind by making a positive contribution to society, through a comprehensive curriculum, dedicated and qualified staff, and adequate facilities within the constraints of fiscal responsibility.

Quite on the other hand, a meaningful mission statement for a school district might read as follows:

The mission of Mapleton Public schools, an innovative, educational system embodying the ideals of the community, is to develop responsible, self-sufficient, creative citizens aware of their own uniqueness and worth by providing a variety of individualized, specialized schools of choice, differentiated by academic and vocational instruction and by delivery systems accommodating various learning styles, that reflect traditional values and enable students to participate in, and effect our changing democratic societies.

Parameters

First, what parameters are not. Parameters, as defined here, are not the traditional board policies; nor the routine, operational, administrative, or academic rules and procedures—like who parks where and how many English credits a student must have to graduate. They are not laws or regulations handed down from the state or local school board. In short, they are not restrictions externally or internally imposed on an organization. And they are not a bilious recitation of the obvious.

Rather, parameters here are strategic parameters: limitations the organization places upon itself for good reason. They are parameters, boundaries in which the organization will operate; they are things the organization either will never do or will always do. Such parameters are "strategic" because they have the effect of "positioning" the organization in terms of its own mission.

Stated usually in the negative, parameters provide a kind of security alarm system to warn the organization when it is about to do something either unwise or dangerous. Stated sometimes in the positive, parameters are the imperatives that keep the organization true to itself. Examples of actual parameters written by school districts indicate the wide variety of parameter content:

• We will not offer any adult or continuing education courses or programs.

- We will accept no new programs or activities without:

  a) a favorable cost-benefit analysis

  b) participation in the development of the program by representatives of all those affected

  c) provision for staff training

  d) a defined evaluation process.

- We will not tolerate any action or circumstances that degrade any person.
- We will develop educational programs and support services in response to community/student needs, rather than staff availability or competence.
- Nothing will take precedence over the Pre-K through 12 instructional program.
- We will not allow parameters, procedures, or behaviors that impede student success.
- We will not employ or retain people who do not subscribe to our beliefs.

There are certain requirements to be met in developing a parameter. First, the parameter must be enforceable and controllable; second, it must be absolutely definitive in its terms; third, it must represent practicality (in any matter, the organization's last practice — not what is written—constitutes parameter).

The notion of parameters is quite often difficult to grasp by planners; but, if properly conceived, parameters are a very critical part of the strategic plan. They can establish "ground rules"; set in place protective mechanisms, rations, formulas, and the like; dictate codes of behavior; define expectations; assert priorities; and define various boundaries. All together, parameters have the effect of focusing the mission statement and of preventing over-zealous pursuit thereof.

Internal Analysis

Strictly speaking, the internal analysis and, for that matter, the external analysis are as much a part of the planning process as of the planning discipline. And while they are not normally included in the final published plan—except, perhaps, as an appendix — they must be considered here as a prerequisite to developing the objectives and strategies, which are the heart of the plan. In fact, it is not unusual for the strategies to be direct responses to these analyses.

That means that honesty is foremost. Complete objectivity, of course, is essential throughout the entire planning process, but it is extremely critical in making these analyses. A failure at this point to deal with all issues openly and frankly will severely detract from the validity of the final plan. On the other hand, forthright analyses produce not only valid objectives and strategies, they also demonstrate to the various publics the organization's sincerity. The internal analysis consists of a thorough, unbiased, tripartite examination of the organization: specifically, strengths; weaknesses; and the organizational design as it reflects responsibility, decision-making and information flow.

Strengths

Strengths are defined as those internal qualities, circumstances, or conditions that contribute to the organization's ability to achieve its mission. For that reason, only those strengths that directly relate to the stated mission should be considered here. That is to say, emphasis should not be on strengths relative to other like organizations, but strictly relative to this local mission.

A recognition of strengths is important in planning because it signals to the organization the areas in which success may be most easily compounded. Real strengths represent achievement and, therefore, are testimony to the organization's ability to perform, as well as its potential for even greater achievement. In fact, excellence is nothing more than a strength pursued to its ultimate.

A typical list of a school district's strengths reads like this:

- Child-focused staff
- Excellent fiscal management
- Community participation
- Strong volunteer program
- Excellent early intervention and Child Find programs
- High student achievement measured by test scores
- Exemplary special educational programs
- Affirmative Action Plan
- High level of trust within management
- Rapport with State Department of Education
- Credibility at state level
- Excellent employee benefits
- Numerous scholarships, awards, and recognitions for our students
- Parent involvement/support

- Performance-based curriculum
- People willing to take risks.

Weaknesses

The weaknesses of an organization are those internal characteristics, conditions, or circumstances that restrict, or even prevent, the realization of the mission. Whereas strengths represent achievement, weaknesses usually indicate either a lack of performance or the inability to perform. However, weaknesses are quite often simply the result of benign neglect. Therefore, they are not necessarily a reflection of the abilities or the intent of the organization, but of either its priorities or its current capacity.

There is one very important thing to remember about weaknesses: That is, all organizations have them and will continue to have them. The trick is to distinguish between those weaknesses that are tolerable and those that are critical. That is to say, some weaknesses can be, and sometimes must be, lived with; it is a waste of resources and much weariness of the flesh to attempt to overcome them. Organizations that attempt to do this are majoring in minors. But critical weaknesses—those which negatively affect the realization of the mission—must, quite obviously, be identified for correction. That corrective action will be reflected in the objectives and strategies.

Typical weaknesses listed by a school district are:

- Board decision versus administrative interpretation leads to confusion
- Differences in management styles leading to inconsistent application of parameters
- Unclear instructions given from administration to building principals to volunteers
- Unclear accountability/responsibility at all levels
- Important decisions made in isolation without known criteria
- The district is not a good communicator between parents and community at large
- Inequity among buildings (facilities, supplies, books, etc.)
- Not enough qualified substitute teachers
- Weak communication between administration and local and state government agencies
- General salary inequities

- Disproportionate time and energy spent on small numbers of students
- "Sloppy" staff work
- Inefficient office procedures (lack of computerization)
- Too many layers between superintendent and principals
- Too many special interest groups running their own agenda
- Some people involved in curriculum development are not taking an active role or providing active leadership
- Building and departmental supply budgets are inadequate to meet classroom teachers' needs
- Salary compensation inadequate for some classroom positions when compared to responsibilities
- Too much dead weight/ inconsistent treatment by administrators of inadequate employees
- "Low-bid mentality."

Organizational Critique

The third part of the internal analysis is the critical analysis of organization; that is, a close examination of the organization's internal functions, communication, and systems of accountability and authority as reflected in the organizational design. This critique is not aimed at correcting; merely at determining what is working and what is not. In fact, at this point, "fixes" or solutions are totally inappropriate. For this reason the very last thing that will be done in the planning process is a strategic organization (or reorganization). Why? Because one of the cardinal principles of strategic management is this: organize to the plan; do not plan to the organization.

Translated into practice, this means that organizing cannot properly take place until the final and complete plan is set. Then, and only then, is the organization arranged for implementation. But a thorough critique at this point in the planning process not only identifies the present difficulties that need to be remedied, but also establishes a somewhat philosophical context — if not rationale — for future organizing.

The traditional organizational design that is, the hierarchical arrangement, must be approached from five points of view: (1) span of control; (2) layers; (3) gaps; (4) redundancies; and (5) formality versus informality.

"Span of control" refers to the number of people or functions that report to

64

any one person. The fact is that there is a limit to what a person can effectively manage; beyond that point there is a loss of control. While the old rule of thumb is five to seven subordinates; in actual practice, effective span of control is determined by many variables other than numbers. For example, the abilities of both the manager and subordinates; the type of work involved; the geographical spread or the physical layout of the work; and the organization's management philosophy are all factors influencing, and even sometimes dictating, span of control. A typical example of the kind of observations that might constitute the critique of span of control is: "The assistant superintendent for instruction has fifty-one subordinates reporting directly."

"Layers" has reference to the number of levels in the organization; that is, the graduations of authority from top to bottom. This aspect of an organization is critical because of its intrinsic relationship to decision making. Usually, the more layers, the longer the process. In fact, it is possible through layering to substitute process for decision. And when layering is further compounded by dotted lines running here and there throughout the organizational chart, there is clear evidence that the organization is designed not around specific authorities for decision making with the accompanying accountabilities, but rather to obscure accountability through deliberate vagueness in individual responsibility, thereby rendering decision making (as well as results) irrelevant. In fact, dotted lines are a clear indication that the organization does not know what anyone is doing. Layering must be evaluated strictly in terms of its effect on the functioning of the organization. An example of an observation dealing with verticality might be: "The department heads must go through six levels of management for approval to purchase classroom equipment," or, "The associate superintendent carries the key to the duplicating machine."

"Gaps" and "redundancies" are quite similar in the sense that they both represent the inappropriate application of resources to task. But they are different in that one means too little; the other, too much. Specifically, "gaps" in the organization's structure occur when functions vital to the mission are not translated into actual jobs, authority, or reporting relationships. That is to say: (1) There is no position charged with the function; (2) there is a position, but it lacks authority to function; or (3) there is a position with appropriate authority, but it is relegated to ineffectiveness by short-circuited relationships with other parts of the organization. An example of a gap is: "We have no public

Category: *Economic*		
Factors	**Predictions**	**Impact**
1. *Public School Revenue*	1. A. General fund revenue mandated by formula from state	1. A. a. Limits programs b. Limits staff c. Limits supplies/ materials d. Affects class size e. Possible school closures/inc. busing f. Reduced building maintenance
	B. Board choice to hold budget/bond election	B. a. Revenues not guaranteed b. Polarizes community

Category: *Economic*		
Factors	**Predictions**	**Impact**
1. *Median Age*	1. A. Percent of population over age 65 will increase	1. A. a. Increase in demand for social service b. Increased competition for tax dollars c. Increase in taxpayer resistance to tax increases for education d. Diminished support e. Availability of senior citizens to community f. Increase in number of potential volunteers g. Significant number of staff retirements h. Replacement of staff increasingly difficult i. Increased demand for adult education j. Increased use of facilities k. Potential for increased alienation between direct consumers of education and the elderly l. More demand for food programs

66

relations office," or, "Everyone coordinates staff development, so there is no staff development." Gaps usually are the major cause of management by swarm.

"Redundancies" simply means that a job or task is being performed or supervised by more than one person or more than one organizational unit, without good reason. Not only does this result in expensive duplication of effort, but it also obscures responsibility and accountability, because anybody's job is nobody's job; or, perhaps more to the point, if two people are equally responsible for the same thing, neither is. In practice, co-responsibility means no accountability. In short, redundancy means that a decision is being made more than once, and an activity is being performed more than once, without good reason. A typical example of a redundancy is: "The affirmative action program is being administered by three offices."

The final organizational analysis is simply a comparison (or contrast) of the organizational chart and the actual functioning of the organization. The greater the difference, the greater the bureaucracy.

If the organization follows non-traditional patterns—that is, anything other than a heirarchy—then the critical analysis must be made on the terms implicit within the design. Specifically, that means what is the intent of the design and how well is it fulfilling its promise. In any case, the assessment of the design must be made based on how effectively it concentrates all energies on the mission and objectives of the enterprise. Efficiency is always a secondary concern.

External Analysis

The external analysis is usually the most exciting part of the planning discipline, because it is futuristic—looking into the future for five to ten years; prophetic—predicting events and conditions that will occur during that time; and challenging—identifying specific impacts on the organization as a result of those events and circumstances. Also appropriately called "environmental analysis," this exercise is based on the realization that there are, and will be, many external factors over which the planning organization has no control; but that does not mean that these external influences must necessarily control the organization. That, in fact, is what planning is all about—maintaining control even in an environment that is out of control.

Stated quite simply, the purpose of the external analysis is to prevent surprises that may negatively affect the organization's ability or opportunity to accomplish its mission. But more than providing mere intelligence about the future, the external analysis may serve as the immediate rationale for the formulation of the strategic commitment of resources. That is to say, the external analysis is not for information only; it is a call to action.

If the external analysis is not complete, it is not worthwhile. And to be complete for school districts, it must deal with at least five categories of influence on the organization: namely, social; demographic; economic; political; technological and scientific; and educational trends and influences. Each category must be analyzed in terms of its several factors, assumptions made about each factor, and the impact of each assumption calculated. For example, in the social category, one district recently identified thirteen factors: language, graying of America, diverse cultures, family structure, sex roles, communicable diseases, job/careers, leisure time, high tech, morals, religion, entertainment, and wellness /appearance.

This raises an interesting point. Most educational leaders have traditionally thought that the best information on subjects such as this come only from big research factories like Harvard Business School, or fancy think-tanks like the Brookings Institution. But the fact is that the external analysis needed for practical planning usually is best performed by the professionals within the organization. Most of them know as much about the future as those paid to study it, and their perception of what the future means to the district has a far more realistic orientation.

The examples on the following pages demonstrate not only the quality of the analyses typically achieved, but also the best format for clarity and effect.

Competition

Somewhat related to the external analysis, but deserving its own special attention for planning purposes, is the matter of competition. Competition is defined as any other organization providing the same goods, products, and services to the same client in a free market-place. Typically, public education has not given a great deal of thought to competition, and certainly not to "products" and the "marketplace." Perhaps that is the reason so many districts are experiencing significant decreases in both enrollment and quality of education. But the fact is that the future of public schools cannot be guaranteed by law; only by the performance of those schools judged against an ever growing number of educational options. In fact, the voucher system and schools of choice, combined with the growing number of for-profit schools, have already forced public education into the free market.

The analysis of competition at this point in the planning discipline forces the district to acknowledge its relative advantages and disadvantages and, furthermore, to consider the points on which the competition is most vulnerable. Some purist educators do not like to talk about things as crass as competition, products, and marketing. But knowledge about competitors may soon prove necessary for survival, certainly for viability.

There are two ways to approach an analysis of competition: one rather complicated, the other simple. The more complicated approach first identifies all the relevant points of comparison and contrast and then looks at each competitor using some sort of value scale. The purpose of this approach is (1) to assess thoroughly the planning district in terms of its competition so plans can be made to strengthen it against competition; and (2) to discover specific weaknesses of each competitor in the event that the planning organization chooses to develop a "marketing" plan either to retain or to gain students. Such an analysis is often charted as follows:

COMPETITION
(Education Organization)

Traits*						
Size						
Image						
Funding						
Expenditure Per Student						
Management						
Quality of Staff						
Curriculum						
Extra Co-curricular Activities						
Teacher-Pupil Ratio						
Etc.						

*Actual figures are used when appropriate; other comparisons will require a numerical scale with values assigned by the planning team. This is not an academic exercise; absolute precision is not required.

The second approach is also very effective, although not quite as thorough or as detailed. It simply identifies the competitor by type (or by name) and then lists the advantages of both the competitor and the planning district, side by side, but not necessarily point for point. Then the competitor's points of vulnerability are listed. Such an analysis typically looks like this:

Competition: *Private/Parochial Schools*	
Their Advantage	**Our Advantage**
Religious education taught	Financial resources
Public perception of small classes	Broad curriculum
	Support services
Elitism/being with own kind	Certificated (highly-qualified staff)
No federal or state mandates	
Sense of ownership because of tuition	More extra curriculum offerings
Perception of caring	Better/broader plant facilities
Parents feel they have more control	More diverse staff and students
Can select their students	Broader base of support
	More up-to-date equipment/ texts and curriculum research
	Accredited course work
	External/internal technical assistance
	Total community input
	No tuition

Points of vulnerability: Inferior staff qualifications. Inadequate texts, equipment, and facilities. Increasing costs for them.

Once the analysis of competition is complete, the organization has all the information needed to develop appropriate transformational objectives and strategies to support the mission statement. From this point forward, the planning discipline consists strictly of decision making.

Critical Issues

At this juncture in the planning discipline, quite often it is helpful to identify critical issues; that is, areas in which the institution faces the prospect of getting either much worse or much better. As noted earlier, "crisis" is the point between life and death, success or failure. Critical issues, therefore, are those issues that must be dealt with if the organization is to survive or to recreate itself in the context of its own stated mission. Usually, these critical issues can be identified only by a thorough reconsideration of the beliefs, the parameters, the internal and external analyses, and the assessment of competition.

Identifying the critical issues focuses attention on the paramount threats and opportunities, and thereby provides a compelling rationale for the strategic deployment of resources. Threats are negative and inevitable; in the extreme, they disable or destroy. Opportunities are those blessings of time and circumstance that are uniquely those of the organization because of what it is, where it is, and when it is. And there is always just one best opportunity for truly creating a new an organization. This is the only way to metamorphosis.

Objectives

The statement of objectives is the planning organization's commitment to achieve specific, measurable end results. In essence, the objectives are tied very closely to the mission statement; in fact, they both spring from and define the mission. These are not administrative objectives, operational objectives, nor even building objectives: They are district objectives.

Quite simply, the objectives are what the organization must achieve if it is to accomplish its mission and be true to its beliefs. Such objectives are the specification of the mission into results. Therefore, objectives should be student-centered.

In fact, district strategic objectives logically deal only with student achievement, student performance, or student success before and after graduation. Both prudence and good planning demand that the number of objectives be limited. Typically, three or four objectives, if properly written, will capture the vision and stretch required to realize the mission.

Most school districts have great difficulty writing suitable objectives because most educators seem to be more process oriented than result oriented. So most educational planners seem to resist the one requirement of an objective: That is, it must be measurable, demonstrable, and observable. If an objective is not measurable, it is not an objective but, rather, a dream or fond hope. The idea of "process objectives" is a figment of an inconsequential imagination. Quite obviously, dreams and hopes are not as intimidating as objectives because they incur no risk and contain no built-in demand for accountability. But true

71

objectives create risks and impose accountability. Quite obviously, the following examples of "objectives" are not only typical namby-pamby dodges of both risks and accountability, but are also good examples of unproductive warm and fuzzy word games:

- To foster community support by providing opportunities for community involvement.
- To provide programs that will maximize student success.
- To provide a well-qualified, effective staff.
- To serve the whole student.

On the other hand, real objectives are commitments to specific significant results in student achievement that are measurable (in terms of quality and quantity), demonstrable, or observable. Examples of such objectives are as follows:

- To graduate 100 percent of our students.
- To have 100 percent of our students, within six months after graduation, either placed in a permanent career or enrolled in an institution of higher learning.
- To have 100 percent of our students achieving at [established] achievement levels.
- To have 100 percent of our students achieving at [expected] grade level.

Strategies

Without doubt, the most important part of the planning discipline and, consequently, of the plan itself is the list of strategies. The strategies, after all, are what makes the plan "strategic." They are, in particular, the articulation of bold commitments to deploy the organization's resources toward the stated objectives. Any and all of the organization's resources—people, facilities, equipment, money—are subject to assignment or reassignment through the strategies.

A "strategy" is not a strategy unless it represents a significant investment toward an expected significant return. Quite obviously, strategies in themselves are indicative of the organization's basic operational emphasis, its priorities, and the standards by which it will measure its own performance.

It is worthwhile noting that the word "strategy" carries primarily a military connotation. In that context, it refers to an optimistic, pre-planned commitment of resources toward an objective: A wise general chooses strategies that can be expected to achieve the desired results at minimum cost, and then puts everything at his command into them to guarantee that success.

Essentially, the strategies tell how the organization will accomplish the objectives, therefore realizing the mission. For that reason, the strategy statements, to be manageable and to allow for a practical flexibility as they are translated into action, must here be conceptualized and stated in rather broad terms. Over-specificity or narrow focus reduces the statements to no more than routine operational details and robs the plan of its authority to establish long-term "positioning" of the organization.

In fact, the first sign of an amateur planner is that he or she will categorize several strategies under each objective. That can only fragment the plan and result in loosely connected, sometimes competing, activities. Rather, each strategy must be broad enough to support and realize each and all objectives.

Only to the degree that the strategies possess inherent power to move the organization along to its predetermined objectives will the organization enjoy control over its own destiny. No power, no control. And the power must reside in the strategies themselves, not in the authorities behind them.

Typical strategies for a school district might read as follows:

- We will develop and support a new comprehensive employee wellness program.
- We will redefine and establish program options for non-college-bound students.
- We will establish a comprehensive results-based staff development program.
- We will develop a teacher-mentor ("master teacher") program.
- We will develop a sequential, comprehensive curriculum for all content areas.
- We will organize strategically to accomplish our mission.
- We will put into effect a consistent and manageable system of job accountability and performance standards.
- We will develop and put in place an individualized, performance curriculum.

Action Plans

The final component of the planning discipline is the action plans. As the name implies, action plans are a detailed description of the specific actions required to achieve specific results necessary for the implementation of the

73

strategies. Each strategy will be developed by several such plans, all containing step-by-step directions, time lines, assignments of responsibilities, and cost-benefit analyses.

It is in the action plans that the strategies become operational. In military terminology, action plans are the "tactics." Correspondingly, each action plan has its own specific objectives and must therefore be judged ultimately on the actual results it produces. Action plans that are long on process and short on getting things done are nothing more than a means of postponing dedicated effort and, hence, a denial of accountability.

The development of action plans seems somehow by nature contrary to the basic disposition of most educators. The overwhelming urge and practice is to plan to plan; and, thereby, it is assumed, to postpone action. But an *action* plan is not a plan to plan. It is, rather, assertion that the requisite detailed planning has been done; all that remains is to get on with the implementation.

Furthermore, it should be pointed out here that the action plans are not to be considered, as some have thought, the implementation portion of the planning process. Action plans are plans and only plans. Developing them does not constitute implementation; having them does not constitute implementation. Neither does talking about them in council meetings from time to time. But it is only by implementing the plans that the strategies will be realized and the objectives achieved. In fact, the action plans are the only component of the strategic plan that will be implemented.

Perhaps the most important characteristic of an effective action plan is that it is conceived and written from an operational point of view. That means that the content is predicated on progressive, direct cause-and-effect relationships and is immediately workable. Action plans should leave little to the imagination and nothing to chance.

While the format of the action plan may vary depending upon content and performance, to be practical it must include at least: (1) specific reference to the strategy it supports; (2) a statement as to the objective of the action plan itself; (3) a detailed description of each step required to accomplish the plan; (4) an indication of assignments and responsibilities; (5) a time line for the plan; and (6) a cost-benefit analysis. Components (4) and (5) will be completed at the beginning of the implementation phase. The recommended

74

format is shown at the end of this chapter.

The cost-benefit analysis that accompanies each action plan is extremely important because such an analysis ultimately forces the question of best use of resources, and the greatest return on investment. For that reason, the degree of accuracy in predicting costs and benefits is the major factor in validating the entire strategic plan in actual performance. That is to say, did the plan produce what it promised at the cost it projected?

There is no single best way to format a cost-benefit analysis. Different undertakings require different methods of explanation; all that is required is that the analysis show what the action will require in both tangible and non-tangible investments, and what the tangible and non-tangible return on investment will be. The recommended format is shown at the end of this chapter.

Summary

With the action plans in place, the strategic planning discipline is complete, and the logical, progressive decision making forced by the discipline is obvious: Beliefs, Mission, Parameters (Internal and External Analyses, Competition, Critical Issues), Objectives, Strategies, and Action Plans. Taken together, the components of the discipline tell "who," "what," and "how"—who the organization is (Beliefs, Mission, Parameters); what it is up to (Objectives); and how it is going to do it (Strategies and Action Plans). Formatted graphically, the discipline looks like this:

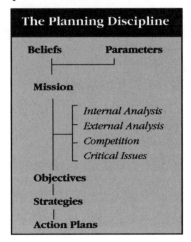

The Planning Discipline

Beliefs   **Parameters**

Mission

  Internal Analysis
  External Analysis
  Competition
  Critical Issues

Objectives

Strategies

Action Plans

Or for those who prefer horizontal charts:

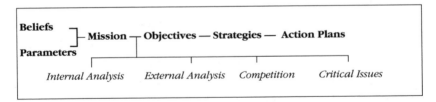

If this appears to be a "model," then it is so only in the nearsighted eye of the beholder. It is, in fact, a fully integrated, dynamic, high-energy discipline by which a significant portion of the future can be created.

ACTION PLAN

SPECIFIC RESULTS:

STRATEGY NO. _____
PLAN NO. _____
DATE: _____

_____
_____

# ACTION STEP *(Number each one)*	Assigned To:	Starting Date:	Due Date:	Completed Date:

Responsible: [_____]

(Shaded areas for management phase)

77

COST-BENEFIT ANALYSIS

COSTS

BENEFITS

Tangible:

Tangible:

Intangible:

Intangible:

(Have you considered opportunity costs and return on investment?)

CHAPTER FIVE

THE PLANNING PROCESS

The planning *process* is essentially "how" the plan is developed — the means, the methods, and the sequence of planning activities. Typically, the process takes approximately nine months to complete and follows a rather rigid, linear course from beginning to end. But, unlike the *discipline*, which is altered only at the peril of seriously weakening the plan, the process quite often must be adapted to local conditions and requirements in order to achieve optimal effect.

Yet, even so, the process must never sacrifice its necessary time-on-task, results-oriented character. Never can it be waylaid by convenience or comfort. And, most important, apparent inconsistency in the process can never be allowed to cast doubt on the credibility of the plan itself. Ideally, any modification in the process outlined here will be made and agreed upon before the actual planning is begun, and set forth as a formatted schedule to which all parties will adhere rigorously. Mid-course changes usually run the risk of both prolonging the process, diluting its substance, and losing credibility. The one cardinal rule of every facilitator and participant should be: "Trust the process."

The Facilitator

The first, and sometimes the most difficult, decision to be made in the planning process is in regard to the facilitator. The necessity of a facilitator is a foregone conclusion; no planning process can be accomplished successfully without this functionary. In fact, the quality of any plan depends first and foremost on the personality, group management skills, and technical knowledge of the facilitator.

The question is whether to use an external or an internal facilitator. That question is not easily resolved because there is not a substantial body of evidence supporting either side. In the private sector, most corporations find, all things being equal, that an external facilitator is more effective in challenging and moving the organization in new directions, as well as imposing the rigors of the planning process on those involved. Even so, most major corporations have a designated full-time "planner" on their staff.

The decision whether to use an internal or external facilitator is strictly a local option, but it must be made carefully, without presupposition, in light of the advantages of either approach.

Briefly, the advantages an *external* facilitator provides are as follows:

1. The professional planner brings an objectivity to the planning process no one inside the organization can possibly enjoy. And this objectivity is necessary if the organization is to: concentrate its attention on the planning process as a serious project—not something someone is handling part-time; face up to critical or sensitive issues in a manner that strengthens relationships and builds mutual self-confidence and *esprit de corps*; and subordinate personal wishes to the good of the organization.

2. The professional planner is more adept at translating the strategic plan into action plans—the point at which most internal planners falter. That is true because no matter how strong the internal planner may be, he or she is still usually identified with his or her own operational responsibility, and usually bailiwicks don't mix.

3. The professional planner, while not a consultant necessarily, is generally a source of "cross-pollination," bringing with him or her to any one organization substantive ideas and techniques that have worked in other instances. His or her academic background, coupled with actual line experience, makes the external facilitator a valuable resource, a provocative catalyst, and a thoroughly unbiased judge of ideas and information.

4. The planning process by its nature excites people and raises their expectations, so it is very important that the process chosen be the one that offers a guarantee of ultimate success. Participants may tend to be disappointed, even a bit cynical, about planning if the first attempt does not meet their expectations.

5. In most instances, the professional planner becomes somewhat of a confidant to the superintendent or chief executive officer of the organization and is able to assist him or her, through the planning process, in identifying and developing management talent.

6. Professional planners do not get paid if they do not produce, and they are more easily fired.

The advantages of an *internal* facilitator are as follows:

1. The internal facilitator is immediately available, so the process can be implemented at the convenience of the school district's calendar. This planner is always present to ensure the long-term commitment to the plan and compliance with the discipline and process of planning.

2. The internal planner is already on the payroll, so additional funds for planning do not become a major obstacle to beginning the process.

3. The internal facilitator is in tune with local issues, concerns, and politics, and so may be able to surface critical matters that may be effectively hidden from an external facilitator.

4. The internal facilitator knows all the players; and the players know the facilitator. Assuming a mutual respect and trust, rapport between facilitator and participants might be more quickly established.

5. The internal facilitator may have planning skills equal to any external facilitator, but that will be true only if the internal planner has had the requisite training and the experience, as well as the commitment to planning as a profession.

Five Important Basics

Perhaps the most important consideration, however, is the internal facilitator's own assessment of his or her role. To be effective, the internal facilitator must meet at least five basic criteria. He or she must:

1. Report directly to the administrative or executive head of the organization; that is, the superintendent.

2. Have been given the sole responsibility for strategic planning; that is, it must be his or her first job—not an additional duty, and not merely assisting someone else who is the "planner."

3. Have been granted the authority to impose upon the organization a rigid work process and to expect strict compliance.

4. Have good group skills, a forceful personality, and technical knowledge of planning.

5. Not value too highly job security. Planning is risky business.

Some districts have found that the most effective facilitation is done by a combination of internal and external facilitators. The external facilitator typically directs the overall process and is directly involved at the beginning and end of the process (first and second planning sessions); while the internal facilitator supervises the planning phase.

Setting a Climate for Planning

No strategic planning project should be undertaken without first establishing a receptive climate. Corporate cultures and institutional bureaucracies are by nature resistant to planning because it threatens the status quo and it challenges personal security. Because school districts typically represent a kind of corporate-institutional hybrid, it is doubly important that the design and intent of the strategic planning project, as well as the details of the planning process, be shared with everyone in the district. Special emphasis should be given to the fact that the process potentially will involve anyone and everyone in the district and that the process inherently contains safeguards against special interest dominance, political manipulation, and basic stupidity.

The most effective communication regarding the planning project comes directly from the superintendent and may be accomplished quite well through all the existing methods or instruments. But the most effective way is a series of special meetings around the district, beginning with the cabinet, to discuss and clarify every aspect of the project.

In addition to communication inside the district, the facilitator or superintendent must wage an intensive effort to inform the community at large about the project. Information packages and interviews should be made available to all the local news media; and, if possible, presentations should be made to civic clubs and other appropriate community groups. Eventually, the strategic planning process will involve and affect the community, so general community awareness and support are invaluable.

System Capacity and Design

Perhaps the most important consideration in preparing for planning is the organization's capacity not only to develop a truly transformational plan but also to implement its own plan. Surprisingly, many corporate as well as educational systems outplan their ability to manage their own creation. The result, of course, is frustration and disappointment.

82

The initial examination of system capacity should not be a detailed analysis of the various components of the system based on correct assessment methodologies or comparison and contrast with other exemplary organizations. Rather, it should begin with an explanation of the current and emerging philosophies regarding human systems—from the traditional corporate model to the natural systems of the "new age." There should be no attempt at this point to choose a specific approach—rather, merely to understand the various philosophies and their implications for the existing organization, and to begin serious thinking about future possibilities While the examination of capacity and design cannot be prescripted, and while solutions at this early stage are premature, the conversation must deal at least with the two basic components of any modern organization—human beings and technology.

Throughout this extended discussion one thing must be made clear: the strategic planning process, not to mention the plan, will leverage the entire school district into an entirely new way of doing business. It can never go back to what it is.

Information Base

The first rule of gathering information regarding the organization and its circumstances is: "Don't overdo it." Strategic planning is not research; it is, rather, decision-making based on adequate but not extensive information. In fact, strategic plans are based more on the collective intuition of the planning team than on so-called hard data. A plethora of minutiae merely confounds. Research has become an end unto itself when it postpones or prevents decisions.

Probably the most effective and efficient way to format organizational information for planning in any organization is "vital" signs. Any human organization, like any human body, has certain health indicators that, when taken together, become a reasonably accurate profile of the organization's total condition and a predictor of its potential for better or for worse. Any professional educator could suggest impromptu a dozen or so such indicators, so there is nothing either revelatory or inclusive about the following list:

- Funding history and prospect
- Enrollment history and projection
- Achievement scores

- Pupil-teacher ratios
- Expenditure per student
- District demographics
- Staff profile
- Salary and benefit comparisons.

Assuming that the organization is developing a five-year plan, each vital sign should be tracked back for the previous five years and then trend-line projected five years into the future. These data will serve during planning as reference points to reality.

Also, if deemed significant, some more qualitative data may be helpful in assessing the less tangible, but equally important, aspects of the district. In no instance should research information or data be allowed to constitute a decision.

The Planning Team

Other than the facilitator, the planning team is the most important factor in the planning process. It is this group that will establish the aspirations and commitments of the organization for years to come and that will monitor, from time to time, the organization's performance toward the plan. Team membership carries with it great honor, but also equally great obligation.

The team must have four characteristics, equally important. First, it must be in composition both strategic and operational, with reference to the organization's design. That is, it must, by its very makeup, mirror the nature of the planning process itself. The entire planning process is a demonstration of the second basic principle of decision-making; specifically, that the "strategic" must be validated by the "operational" and the "operational" must have "strategic" context for meaning. The planning team must reflect the same kind of symbiosis, in that it must be made up of people who have "strategic" responsibility as well as people whose responsibilities are "operational." Exactly where the line of demarcation falls is an academic question. Practically speaking, those drawn at the top of the traditional organizational chart are "strategic"—they are charged by position with establishing overall direction, policies, objectives, and the deployment of resources. Those toward the bottom are more or less responsible for implementation. The planning team has no formal organizational structure and operates without a chairperson. The facilitator must provide that function.

84

Because the team is indeed one for "strategic" planning, the team membership will usually be skewed toward the strategic. Typically, one-third to one-half of the team members will hold strategic responsibilities in the organization. That emphasis is not only proper; it is necessary.

② Second, the planning team must represent every component of the school community. For example, it should include representatives from: administration of every building level, department managers, certified staff from each level (and discipline, if possible), classified staff, community, parents, teachers union, and students. The word "represent" is used here with a very qualified meaning. The team members do not represent their constituents in any political or local sense. They are a part of the team because they are representative of certain values and perspectives that must be taken under consideration if the strategic plan is to be indeed comprehensive and if it is to garner support from throughout the school community.

③ Third, the planning team must be manageable in size. Typically, the planning team consists of twenty to twenty-five members — no more. Usually, in a school district, they are selected from volunteers by the superintendent and the board president with the advice of the facilitator. Selection from volunteers, of course, presupposes that the entire school community has been provided adequate information regarding the purpose and process of the planning activity. The drafting of participants is also appropriate and sometimes necessary to ensure depth and breadth of the team.

As the selection of members is being made, one other required characteristic of the team must be kept paramount — the personality mix. In most districts, it would be possible to put together any number of teams that would meet the strict composition requirements. But mere mechanical ordering of types will guarantee failure. Ultimately, the planning team will develop its own culture, so it is of the utmost importance that each member be (1) a person of good will, (2) articulate, and (3) willing to make decisions by mutual agreement. In the end, there can be no special interests—only common interest; and defensiveness must give way to agreement. In fact, the fourth characteristic of the team is that it is made up of people who are willing to subordinate their own special interests and personal interests to that of the district and the students it serves. After all, consensus is based not on concession, but on conscience.

The First Planning Session

The most significant activity during the entire planing process is the first planning session. During this two and one-half to three days, the planning team develops every component of the planning discipline except the action plans. Essentially, whatever results from this meeting becomes the plan. And even though everything about the plan is still subject to development and testing by the action teams and to approval by the board, each part of the discipline must be approached and concluded with the assumption of finality.

That means that the components of the discipline (beliefs, mission, policies, internal analysis, external analysis, critical issues, objectives, and strategies) cannot be seen as independent or non-sequential entities—but rather as a developmental thought process through which the whole plan evolves. This process must be strictly transformed into the meeting agenda. To alter the order of thought is to risk compromising both the integrity and effect of the plan. While it is desirable, even necessary, to vary the working organizational arrangements of the team, the rational and creative processes, as well as the pace, it must be remembered that unjustified variations or mere cuteness quickly results in distraction and confusion. It also should be noted that, while complication may be a necessary precondition of simplification, simplification is not a necessary consequence of complication.

Facilitation of the Team

The most important function of the facilitator is keeping the team true to the planning discipline. Another sure sign of an amateur facilitator is trusting one's own genius rather than this discipline. The simple fact is, the discipline does not fail; facilitators do.

The second most important function of the facilitator is to keep the team's attention focused on the tasks at hand. The initial planning session must be an isolated, high-intensity, time-on-task concentration of intelligence, energy, and emotion. Experience has proved that far more can be accomplished by this method than by any number of traditional committee meetings held conveniently over several months. Forcing the proceedings into the strict time limitation of thirty to thirty-six hours over three days achieves several results critical to good strategic planning:

1. The total mental immersion in every aspect of the district has a way of

compelling coherence in thinking and also of sparking new thoughts, thus guaranteeing vision.

2. The sense of urgency imposes a necessary judgment on the importance of issues and concerns and separates out those that are not critical to strategic planning, thus engendering boldness.

3. The ardent, prolonged group interaction, along with fatigue, raises the deliberations to a level generally void of pretense, intimidation, and self or special interests, thus assuming sincerity.

4. Time for political manipulation is not available, thus ensuring credibility.

5. The return on effort is manifestly superior to expectations, thus compelling implementation.

The facilitator must be a stern, yet congenial—even charming—taskmaster, exacting compliance to both schedule and group processes, never arguing, never putting forth his or her own views. The facilitator, without becoming overbearing or suppressing participation, must establish from the start his or her control over the group and must maintain that control throughout the planning session. The best control is the facilitator's own example of disciplined behavior and thinking, and commitment to the common purpose of the group. Facilitation is not a role for autocrats, bureaucrats, wimps, or officious poseurs.

The facilitator is, in the highest sense of the word, a "leader;" the role is best served by those who by dint of their own character, commitment, and personality compel others to follow. Unfortunately, anyone who is or who is considered "The Boss" (the superintendent, for example) usually is not effective as a facilitator. The authority invariably gets in the way of both full expression and group agreement; and these two things are vital to the initial planning session.

Challenge and Orientation

The initial planning session is best begun with an evening session, perhaps after dinner, in which the facilitator presents briefly both the "why" and "how" of strategic planning. Typically, the discussion of the urgency for planning will address the various, somewhat global aspects of change, such as: the transition from the information age to the age of biotechnology, the transformation of values, increasing competition in a free market, and evolving demographic trends. The object of this presentation is not as much to inform as to stimulate an appreciation of the scope and possible implications of strategic planning; not to frighten or discourage, but to excite with the discovery of opportunity. After all, the best strategic plans come out of aspiration, not desperation.

The discussion regarding the "how" of planning typically first establishes the basic philosophy of planning; that is, the planners are causes and not effects. The planning team members must feel that they are indeed "change agents."

Then the discussion should provide a brief explanation of both the complete process and the discipline, with particular emphasis on the role of the planning team. The team should know that it is a recommending body without official authority beyond the strength of its own recommendations. Yet, its members must realize the necessity of reaching definite conclusions and providing specific direction for the district. The mere generation of options does not constitute planning. And, finally, the planning team should be made to understand the absolute necessity for an open, honest, participatory approach to its task.

Developing the Components of the Plan

The actual process of the initial planning session depends primarily on the personality and skill of the facilitator, and secondarily on the personality and skill of the team. And the facilitator must seek constantly to adapt each to the other, not merely as the dynamics of the process require, but especially as the process offers opportunity for mutual growth. The best plans evolve correspondingly with the growth of the team toward unity of purpose and effort.

Even so, the entire process must have an overall rigid structure to assure both efficiency and effectiveness. The structure has four dimensions: group sets, group processes, decision-making processes, and timing. "Group sets" refers to the sub-organization of the planning team into at least two variations (or sets) of groups. For this purpose, the group size should be not fewer than five persons, no more than seven. The ideal number is five. And the sets, insofar as possible, should provide a complete differentiation of group memberships.

"Group processes" refers to the progressive interaction of the members of the group toward its objective and the roles that individual members play in the movement of the group (group dynamics). It is extremely helpful if the facilitator can recognize and respond appropriately to the various roles that people play in a group: building, maintenance, and blocking (Appendix One). "Group processes" also refers to the management style demonstrated by the group. It is assumed that all groups will naturally assume a participative style; however, if the group shows signs of succumbing to an autocratic personality or of deteriorating into laissez-faire confusion, the facilitator must provide immediate and pointed counseling. The facilitator must constantly, yet unobtrusively, monitor the working groups in order to guarantee their good progress. Usually, a gentle reminder is enough to get wayward groups back in concert.

"Decision-making processes" of course refers to those commonly accepted rational and creative approaches to either creating or discovering decisions. The traditional rational methods are induction, deduction, and analogy. Among the most popular creative methods are brainstorming, morphological analysis, force fit, brainwriting, visualization (excursion), lists (attributes), lateral thinking (challenge), and convergent and divergent thinking. The planning process, by its nature, demands the extensive use of the creative approaches; however, the creative, if it is to be realized, constantly must be tested, supported, and ultimately proved by the rational. When creativity outpaces innovation, the plan drifts away into fantasy.

"Timing," of course, refers to the order and time limit to which each group task must be subjected. Only one task is exempt; and that is the refining of the mission statement, if necessary, by an *ad hoc* group formed by one member from each of the subgroups. That particular group or groups, works separately from the other proceedings and continues until the total planning team is satisfied with the statement.

The chart on the following page depicts the overall group management recommended for developing the components of the planning discipline.

89

COMPONENT	GROUP SET*	GROUP PROCESS	EFFECTIVE DECISION-MAKING PROCESSES	TIME (HOURS)
Beliefs	5/5 (A)	*Individual to group to team agreement*	Brainstorming Analysis Synthesis	8-10
Mission	5/5 (A)	*Individual to group to team agreement*	Visualization Divergent & lateral thinking Lists	2-3
(Mission Refinement)*		*Agreement Synthesis*	Assimilation	Variable
Internal Analysis (Mission)*	5/5 (B)	*Individual to group to team general agreement*	Analysis	3-5
External Analysis (Mission)*	5/5 (B)	*Group to team awareness*	Analysis Induction Deduction Divergent thinking	4-6
Critical Issues (Mission)*	5/5 (A)	*Awareness agreement*	Visualization Divergent thinking	2-3
Objectives	5/5 (A)	*Group to team agreement*	Force-fit Lateral thinking Visualization	2-4
Parameters	5/5 (A)	*Agreement*	Brainstorming Analysis	2-3
Strategies	5/5 (A)	*Group to team agreement*	Convergent thinking Visualization	3-4

Based on a team of 25

Communicating the Plan

The success of a strategic plan depends upon its credibility among the total organization. The best way to guarantee that credibility, assuming the efficacy of the plan itself, is immediate, full, and open presentation of every component of the plan as it has been drafted by the planning team to everyone involved in the organization. Quite likely, even prior to the selection of the planning team, the strategic planning project received considerable publicity both inside and outside the organization. And the initial planning session created a great deal of interest, curiosity, and perhaps even some anxiety. So, the sooner the results of that session can be made public, the better.

In larger districts, this is accomplished internally by a series of round-robin meetings at strategic locations. In smaller districts, perhaps a single presentation at a general convocation is more appropriate. The facilitator or the superintendent, or both, should make the presentation. It is highly desirable that a board member from the planning team and other team members be present.

Every component of the plan, exactly as developed by the planning team, should be shown (by overhead projector, power-point, or video) and discussed; usually it is not generally distributed. After all, this is a draft of the plan, and as such, should not be subjected to mass undisciplined scrutiny of its particulars. The ensuing process will allow for full examination and critique, but in appropriate ways and by responsible people. A general distribution at this point runs the risk of ideas and statements being taken out of context and thus distracting productive effort by inconsequential wrangling over details.

If the decision is made to distribute the plan, as some districts have done, only the beliefs, mission, policies, objectives, and strategies should be disseminated—never the internal or external analyses.

A special courtesy presentation of the plan should be made at this time to the board of education. However, this presentation is for its information only. It must not be taken as an occasion for the board to critique, approve, or disapprove. The board must willingly suspend its judgment until the plan is complete in every respect and is submitted in final draft for approval.

Building Action Teams

The communication of the plan to the various constituents of the organization is necessary not only to guarantee the immediate and accurate flow of information, it also serves as an opportunity to solicit members for the action teams. At each presentation of the plan, the facilitator should discuss the formation of action teams (one for each strategy), the teams' critical role in the development of the plan, and the manner in which the teams will be selected. At the conclusion of each presentation, the opportunity should be provided for persons to volunteer to serve and to express a preference as to strategy assignment. The facilitator may also find it desirable to actually conscript certain people to serve on the team.

When all the names and preferences are collected, the planning team (or, more likely, an *ad hoc* group from the team) meets to put together the action teams and to designate the action team leaders. Of course, they should honor individual preferences as much as possible, but the main purpose of this exercise is to build strong, objective, committed teams who are a sort of "mini" version (typically, 10 to 25 members) of the planning team itself. Here again, the credibility of the planning process is of paramount concern. For that reason, members of the strategic planning team may serve on action teams, but should not be action team leaders. Also, teams obviously dominated by special interests or riddled with perceived incompetence are automatically suspect and, consequently, disregarded by others in the district.

The final action teams' membership and leadership should be approved by the superintendent and the board.

Action Team Work

The action team phase of the planning process is critical to the strategic plan. In fact, this is probably the most important phase of the planning process. It is during this time that specific, operational plans of action are developed to implement the strategies. A failure here means a failure of the strategy. The action teams will not implement the plans, but the plans they develop will contain such specific detail that they can be easily carried out when operationally assigned. That means that the plans cannot be just "plans to plan," but outlines of specific, detailed actions necessary to accomplish the strategy. Typically, each strategy will require two to three dozen plans.

The action teams begin their work only after the facilitator has provided the team leaders, usually as a group, with comprehensive and detailed instruction regarding the action teams' responsibilities. Usually accomplished in a three-to-six-hour session, the instruction includes: (1) the role of the action team leader, (2) the relationship between the strategies and the action plans, (3) an explanation of the action plan form, (4) an explanation of cost-benefit analysis, (5) the relationship of the action teams to the planning team regarding final approval of the action plans, and (6) the time commitment usually required (typically, thirty hours of meeting time—at convenient intervals of one-to three-hour sessions—plus an indeterminate amount of time outside meetings). If specific training or instruction is required by any or all of the team leaders, the facilitator should see that it is provided as soon as possible. For example, quite often the facilitator will recognize a need for training the team leaders in group processes or decision-making.

It is particularly critical that the action team leader understand that the action team must honor the strategy exactly as it is written. That is, the action

92

team must accept the strategy with the full intention of making it work—not with the intent to change or eliminate it. However, if it turns out that, after demonstrated good faith effort, the strategy must be altered, then the action team is duty-bound to make the appropriate recommendations to the planning team through the facilitator and, upon approval, proceed to develop the revised strategy.

The first meeting of each action team should produce a general time line for the team's activities, an outline of possible action plans they will pursue, and any internal organization of the team according to tasks. Notes or minutes from this meeting and all subsequent meetings should be forwarded to the facilitator. The teams will be allowed to steer a rather independent course, adopt their own management style, and conduct their activities at the convenience of the group. Each team should be encouraged by the facilitator to work in isolation from the other action teams; there should be no attempt to coordinate or merge activities or plans. If any consolidation is appropriate, it will be done by the planning team at its second session.

During the three or four months the action teams are at work, the facilitator must effectively monitor, discipline, stimulate, and support the teams' efforts. Some of the ways the facilitator functions during this time include: (1) coordinating meeting times and places for all teams, (2) providing various clerical and other support services, (3) arranging for release time or additional compensation, and (4) being available to answer specific questions or provide personal assistance when necessary. Most importantly, the facilitator must meet formally with each team (or team leader) once each month to assess progress and to project upcoming requirements. Finally, the facilitator must ensure that the action plans and cost-benefit analyses submitted by each team are in the appropriate form for submission to the planning team.

The Second Planning Session

At the conclusion of the action planning phase, the planning team conducts its second and final session (two to three days) to put into draft form the complete strategic plan. This session does not demand the physical isolation that was so crucial to the first session; nevertheless, the meeting should be held off-campus at some convenient, neutral site. Nor does the intensity of this meeting equal that of the first. The pace is slower, more deliberate, but still subject to the discipline of a fairly strict schedule.

The first order of business is to review all the action plans that have been submitted by the action teams. Ideally, the members of the planning team have each received a complete package of the action plans, along with evaluation forms, at least one week before the session; so the review should proceed apace. To facilitate the review, each action team leader makes a scheduled appearance (one hour or so) before the planning team to clarify, explain, or justify the team's recommendations. The team leaders do not attend any other portion of this session.

Usually, the planning team is well advised to withhold any comment on, and especially any evaluation of, the plans until all have been presented by the action team leaders. Reserving judgment saves time and ego and contributes mightily to the quality of the final product.

After all presentations have been made, the planning team then begins its assessment of each plan and through consensus makes a final disposition of every one. Since the planning team alone is ultimately responsible for developing a realistic, visionary strategic plan, the team has several options regarding disposition of any and all of the action plans:

- It can accept a plan *carte blanche*.
- It can reject a plan outright.
- It can send a plan back to the action team for further development.
- It can reject any part of a plan and accept the rest.

There are two things the planning team cannot do. The first thing the planning team *cannot* do is put any plan on hold; each and every one must be dealt with by some definitive action. The second thing the planning team *cannot* do is change or add to an action plan; planning teams do not write action plans.

In addition to reviewing and selecting action plans to support the strategies, the planning team usually finds this an appropriate time to review again every component of the plan (starting with *beliefs*), just to confirm its own satisfaction with the content and coherence of the total plan.

The final task of the planning team is to develop a recommended schedule of implementation for the strategies and plans, including a year-by-year cost projection. Usually, this is put in rough draft by the entire planning team, refined by a smaller *ad hoc* group working with the finance director, and approved by the entire team before submission to the board, via the superintendent, as a part of the plan.

As with the first planning session, the planning facilitator is the person who is responsible first, for moving this planning session to the necessary ends; second, for the construction and validation of the implementation and cost schedule; and third, for transforming everything into a final draft ready for board consideration.

Board Approval

One critical point: Prior to submission of the plan to the board, the facilitator must observe two serious matters of protocol, if not obligation. The first is the appraisal of all the action teams as to the final disposition of their recommendations, and the dissolution of the teams. This can be accomplished most easily by a review meeting with the action team leaders who in turn can inform their respective teams and, at the same time, announce the dissolution of the action teams. The second responsibility of the facilitator is the submission of the total strategic plan to the superintendent for his or her final review before presentation to the board. This should be a mere formality because of the superintendent's active involvement in every part of the planning process, but the plan should not be submitted to the board without the commitment of a formal endorsement by the superintendent.

Sometimes the presentation of the strategic plan to the board is made by the facilitator at the behest of the superintendent, usually in two study sessions. Of course, both the planning team and the action teams should be encouraged to attend these sessions, but only the planning team should be granted the status of "official" access to the board, and then only in response to board inquiry through the facilitator. There must not be any direct interaction between the board and individuals speaking as action team members. The plan under consideration is the property and the recommendation of the planning team and should be dealt with accordingly.

Very seldom does a board significantly alter any portion of the plan. That is not to say that it merely "rubber stamps" it, but its quick and full approval is merely evidence of both the quality of the plan and the effective communication that has existed throughout the entire process. It is the facilitator's job to make sure the board is neither painted into a corner nor surprised.

Implementation

Most strategic plans that fail do so at the point of implementation. The whole intent of strategic planning is to translate strategic intent into strategic action, but that inevitably proves to be an exceedingly difficult and sometimes impossible undertaking. It is so for a variety of reasons: inertia, resistance, operational distractions, and confusion of responsibilities—just to mention a few.

The first requirement for successful implementation, assuming a workable plan, is the emphatic and relentless support of the plan from those with strategic responsibilities, particularly the chief officer. Strategic plans rise and fall with the leading of the superintendent. The superintendent must view strategic planning as the overarching *schema* that provides the context for all existing and proposed activities within the district, and everything must be judged by its contribution to the current plan.

Furthermore, in an even larger context, the superintendent and board, probably along with others—administrators, teachers, students, parents— must begin to make serious judgments as to the kind of organization design most appropriate for the district. Of critical concern, of course, is the question as to how and where decisions are made. One approach is simply to create an organization design based on whatever premise and then bring everything and everybody into compliance with that form—*a la* the corporate model. A far better approach is the creation of a system whose organization is dynamic, flexible, undrawable. This concept makes organization a means, not an end. It can be accomplished only through the practice of mutual expectations, conscientiously established and religiously followed.

So, the second essential requirement in translating plans into action is the thorough fusion of the action plans into the mutual expectations of all personnel. This process achieves two results, one quite serendipitously. The first, obviously, is that every action plan is taken by someone for implementation; the second is that, if properly structured, the process offers an excellent means of developing objective performance expectations and consequent performance evaluations, rather than the sneaky, subjective mish-mash which passes—so often argumentatively—as employee evaluation. The first is the concern of the facilitator. The second should be the concern of the superintendent because, if properly carried out, the resulting accountability system would ensure that everything done in the district is consistent with and supportive of the district's mission and objectives and can be assessed in terms of its contribution thereto. At this point strategic planning becomes strategic organization.

Admittedly, this approach is not very popular in organizations given to process rather than results. One bright, young high school principal, when confronted with the prospect of accountabilities, remarked to his colleagues, "I will not write down anything today for which I will be held accountable later." This comment may reveal more about the plaintiff. Without strict mutual expectations, the strategic plan very quickly becomes a mere adjunct to "normal" operation, and action plans assigned otherwise are usually considered just one of many "other duties as assigned." Quite simply, as the high school principal stated, nothing will be done.

There is a real, philosophical debate over the use of mutual expectations in this fashion. One significant body of opinion holds that job descriptions of all administrators should be fast and secure in a filing cabinet, the strategic plan in another; and that the two should never meet. The fact is that, unless one is translated into the other, via prior mutual expectations, there exist neither accountability nor strategic plan.

The most effective, though not least painful, way to accomplish this is through the use of a very simple form which identifies four aspects of each person's job: (1) all job components, (2) results or rationale associated with each component, (3) performance expectations in each result area, and (4) the system support required to accomplish the specific expectations.

The development of these expectations should proceed, under the direction of the facilitator, like this:

- Specific action plans are accepted by the appropriate person (this step may be accomplished at any time in the process).
- Each person, with the assistance of the planning facilitator, identifies what should be his or her own job components—the total range of domain and relationships.
- Each person states the basic rationale (results) associated with each component, in measurable, demonstrable, or observable terms.
- Each person identifies the specific performance expectations in each result area, being careful to note when applicable the specific action plan to which the objective applies.

97

- Each person negotiates to establish specific "prior mutual expectations" of individual performance and system support.

Periodic Updates

Once the expectations are agreed upon, then quarterly reviews should be held to assess both individual performance and the progress of the plan. These reviews should be conducted for all persons by all those involved. But the purpose of the reviews should not be to "evaluate" performance in the traditional sense of the word; it is, rather, to adjust performance to the expectations and, if necessary, the expectations to the performance. It must always be remembered that any evaluation of a person's performance is an evaluation of the whole system.

Effective quarterly reviews are the most expeditious means of both realizing and controlling the strategic plan. If these reviews are properly structured and carried out, the superintendent, the facilitator, and everyone else in the district will know at any given time the status of any given action plan and its strategy. That allows the superintendent and other administrators, including the board, to manage to the strategic plan, and that is tantamount to the total concentration of effort on the mission and objectives of the district. And that, after all, is what strategic planning is supposed to be.

Strategic planning is not an event; it is a way of life for any successful organization. That is why periodic updates of the strategic plan are vital not only to the plan but to the organization itself. In fact, the first annual update is the most important part of the planning process for several reasons. First, the fact that it occurs represents a genuine commitment to strategic planning; so, if there is any lingering hope that it might simply go away as other fads, that notion is dashed. Second, by subjecting the plan to a new reality, it achieves a revalidation of priorities and is strengthened in credibility. Third, because much of the plan will have been already accomplished, it generally gains a narrower focus which means even more intense concentration of effort on probably even more significant objectives. And fourth, the first update should be scheduled to allow the planning process to get in sync with the budgeting process; so, from this year on, the organization should be able to budget its plan, not plan its budget.

The process of the updates is very similar to the initial planning session. The original planning team, or a reasonable facsimile, meets for two to three days in seclusion and, under the guidance of the facilitator, follows a slightly modified version of its first session. The same components of the plan are addressed; the major difference is that components are developed in a different order. Typically, the annual update proceeds as follows:

1. Internal analysis (with emphasis on the changes in the past year and anticipated changes during the next year)
2. External analysis (with emphasis on changes in the past year and anticipated changes during the next year)
3. Critical issues
4. Review of beliefs
5. Review and revision of mission
6. Review and revision of parameters
7. Review and revision of objectives
8. Review of current strategies
9. Drafting of new strategies.

Of course, as the reviews are conducted, revisions, deletions, and additions are made as appropriate.

Should additional strategies be written, as they most assuredly will be, they are assigned to action teams, as before, for development. The process from that point through implementation is merely a condensed version of the first, managed for the most part by the planning facilitator, but made operational as soon as possible.

If the process of strategic planning is viewed as a continuing creative experience, the concept of strategic organization becomes a reality; and the driving force of the system becomes its own intent. Some say it's risky business; but it's not half as risky as the alternative.

CHAPTER SEVEN

SCHOOL/SITE PLANNING

Although the concept is at least two decades old, there still remains considerable interest in site-based management (also known as school-based management, building-based management, and school-centered decision-making). Buoyed by research that champions the school as the fundamental unit of change, principals are clamoring to increase decision-making responsibility at the school level. Advocates justify site-based management on two beliefs: (1) Those most closely affected by decisions ought to play a significant role in making those decisions; and (2) educational reform efforts will be most effective when implemented by people who feel a sense of ownership and responsibility for developing reform initiatives.

Although there are compelling reasons to endorse the idea of site-based management, local boards of education have traditionally been concerned that site-based management undermines the authority of elected lay governance of public schools. Local boards are not just interested in effective schools. They are responsible for effective school systems. Local boards expect an effective school system to be greater than the sum of its individual parts. Consequently, board members often fear that accepting site-based management means abdicating legal responsibility for the entire system.

Site-Based Management: The Decentralization Dilemma

The current interest in site-based management is a recent manifestation of the decentralization-centralization debate. This debate is not new nor is it confined to school districts. All large complex organizations must address questions concerning who should make which decisions.

Decentralizing decision-making becomes a viable option as an organization grows and becomes more complex. As an organization grows, it becomes more difficult to make all the important decisions in one centralized location. As an organization becomes more complex, it becomes more difficult for a few key leaders to be the most knowledgeable experts in all phases of the operation. To cope with growth and complexity, decisions have to be shared with a larger pool of people and the pressure to decentralize mounts.

The primary problem in the decentralization dilemma is: How do you manage effectively from afar? On the one hand, it is inefficient to continue to make all the key decisions in a centralized location. Doing so stifles initiative and greatly reduces the ability to respond quickly. If all decisions are made by people occupying positions at the top of the organizational chart, people throughout the organization feel powerless over their professional destiny.

On the other hand, allowing others decision-making discretion weakens control of top management. It also potentially loosens adherence to quality control standards. How do leaders in an organization continue to maintain control of the organization without stifling individual initiative? How do they ensure individuals are working toward the organization's objectives without dampening motivation?

For school districts, the key decentralization questions are:

1) Which decisions must be made centrally and implemented uniformly in all the schools of a district?

2) Which decisions are more appropriate to make at the school site?

Few districts are either totally decentralized or centralized. Some decisions must be centralized. Without common direction, there really is no organization. There is only an aggregate of individuals pursuing their own ends without coordination or restraint. Other decisions should be decentralized. Sharing decisions with people who have responsibility for implementing those decisions increases motivation.

Consequently, it would be a mistake to assume that decentralization/ centralization is an either/or proposition within any district. Success depends upon people reaching consensus on which decisions are to be made by whom and then faithfully implementing those decisions.

Setting Direction and Decentralization

The decentralization-centralization dilemma is as important in terms of setting an organization's future direction as it is for operational decisions. Who is responsible for setting direction? Should there be common direction for the entire district set by the board of education? Or should each principal be responsible for setting future direction for each individual school?

On the surface, the answers to these two questions appear to be mutually exclusive. Developing a strategic plan for the district is a centralizing force; developing school/site plans is a decentralizing force. In reality, however, this is only an apparent paradox. Developing a strategic plan for the district and site-based plans for each school can be mutually supportive. If done appropriately, developing both strategic and school/site plans creates the synergy necessary to transform a local school system. This synergy will not exist if either is absent. School/Site plans developed without a district's strategic plan are recipes for fragmentation. Furthermore, a strategic plan without complementary school/site plans will be hollow and lack passion. By first developing a strategic plan for the district, and then developing complementary school/site plans, a school system can appropriately resolve decision-making issues related to the district's long-term direction and help it achieve its mission.

For school-based planning to work effectively, school staff must recognize that the school district is the strategic unit. As subdivisions of state government, the local board of education has been vested with statutory authority. As elected representatives of the people, the board has legitimate authority to set direction for the school district.

To ensure effective implementation, however, districts must recognize that schools are the chief operational units in a school system. Everything important that happens to students in a school district, happens in a school—not at the district office. None of the decisions made at the central office matter if schools cannot translate intent into quality programs and services for students.

Importance of District-Wide Strategic Plan

Because the district is the strategic unit in a local school system, the district needs to develop a strategic plan to shape the direction of the entire system. District-wide strategic direction is necessary for two reasons. First, the district needs to establish and maintain standards. These standards are the measures of effectiveness for the schools. Second, the district must ensure equitable distribution of resources throughout the district. The strategic plan provides common direction for every school within a district. It provides the conceptual guidance for creating the future of the entire system, as well as for each of the system's parts.

The district's strategic plan defines the context within which school/sites must operate and develop their plans. It provides the context that is necessary to ensure responsible decentralization. Without the district plan, people in schools have no frame of reference for determining the appropriateness of their actions. In other words, the district's strategic plan legitimizes plans developed at the local school site.

Importance of School/Site Plans

Using the district's strategic plan as background information, each school should develop a site-specific plan that complements the district plan. School/Site plans promote responsible autonomy by allowing people at the local level to develop and implement plans within the district's framework. It is through the school/site plans that the dreams expressed in the district's strategic plan are transformed into reality for students in their schools.

Developing school/site plans unleashes the creative power and energy of people throughout the system to implement initiatives identified in the strategic plan. The passion for planning tends to be greatest at the school level. Whereas districts are abstractions to most people, schools are "real" organizations which motivate people to extraordinary effort in order to make a difference in the lives of students. Motivation and enthusiasm for achieving excellence are greater when developing school/site rather than strategic plans. When the school/site plans are developed within the context of a district's strategic plan, meaningful improvement is possible throughout a school system.

Developing School/Site Plans

The discipline and process for developing a strategic plan can be modified appropriately to develop complementary school/site plans. When developing school/site plans, planners should adhere to three guidelines:
1. School/site plans must be consistent with the district's strategic plan.
2. School/site plans must actively contribute to achieving the mission, objectives, and strategies in the strategic plan.
3. School/site plans must be able to focus on pressing issues that need to be addressed at that particular site.

The first two guidelines are messages directed at staff who work in the schools.

As school/site plans are developed, they must not be in conflict with the district's plan. In other words, schools cannot operate in a manner inconsistent with the district's beliefs and mission and they must operate within the strategic parameters in the district's plan.

Schools must also actively contribute to achievement of the district's mission, objectives, strategies, and action plans. This is a much higher standard to meet than merely to be consistent with the district's plan. Together, adherence to these two guidelines tightens the linkages between the common direction set forth in the district's strategic plan and how schools actually operate. They provide assurance that all of the parts (schools) in a school system are moving in the same direction as the whole system.

The third guideline for developing school/site plans is a caution directed at the board, superintendent, and central office staff. The district's strategic plan cannot be so large and all encompassing that local schools have no resources left to address issues that are specific to them. When a decision is made to develop school/site plans, care should be exercised to limit the district's strategic plan to only those objectives, strategies, and action plans that are applicable throughout the entire district. This will permit schools the flexibility to develop plans that address issues specific to that site, as well as assist with implementation of district initiatives. If the strategic plan is too large, school staff will be frustrated that their resources are stretched to the limit implementing district directives, with no time or energy remaining to address local school problems.

Developing school/site plans helps a district clearly define decision-making responsibilities as well as empower people at the school level to work for meaningful change. Adherence to these three guidelines for developing school/site plans will help districts appropriately balance district and school concerns in their strategic planning.

Components of Strategic and School/Site Plans

Although the components of a school/site plan are very similar to those in the district's strategic plan, there are two important differences. First, a separate beliefs statement should not be developed for each school. If the belief statement in the strategic plan was developed correctly, the district's beliefs represent convictions of the entire organization, not ones that vary from school to school. Second, it is not necessary to develop parameters as part of a school/site plan. The following chart identifies the components of each type of plan.

PLAN COMPONENTS	
District Strategic Plan	**School/Site Plan**
1. Beliefs	1. Mission Statement
2. Mission Statement	2. Internal Analysis
3. Strategic Parameters	3. External Analysis
4. Internal Analysis	4. Objectives
5. External Analysis	5. Tactics
6. Objectives	6. Action Plans
7. Strategies	
8. Action Plans	

Although each school does not develop a separate statement of beliefs, each site's planning team should review and fully understand the district's statement of belief s. At a minimum, school planning teams should discuss why each belief was included in the district's plan, as well as how closely that school's actions are aligned with the organization's beliefs.

Whether or not individual schools develop parameters as part of a school/site plan is best determined at the local level. Developing school/site parameters seems to be a case of overkill. Parameters, by definition, are self-imposed limitations. Schools are already restricted by state law, board policy, negotiated agreements, and the district's strategic plan. Considering the number of existing limitations, it seems silly to impose yet another set at the individual school site. However, if a school planning team believes it is necessary to establish guidelines for operation that are applicable at that site, they should be allowed to do so.

Each school should develop a specific mission statement. Because elementary, middle, and high schools serve different clients with different needs, developing school missions provides the opportunity for clearly defining the market niche for each school.

Each school's mission should pass the usual tests for a mission statement. It should be written in one sentence and include both purpose and function. It also must pass the additional test of being consistent with the district's mission.

An internal analysis is essential in a school/site plan. Strengths and weaknesses are identified in the same manner as in the district's strategic plan. Now, however, those characteristics describe the specific school rather than the entire district.

For a school/site external analysis, the political and economic categories should be replaced by a category entitled central office. For a school, the central office is the external force that defines the school's political and economic reality. The other categories in the external analysis: social, demographic, educational, and technological factors should be analyzed in terms of their impact directly on the school.

Once the internal and external analyses are completed, the school planning team should set objectives for the school. Like the district's objectives, school objectives should be written as long-term end results which, if achieved, would ensure the school would be closer to achieving its mission. Furthermore, to ensure each school is also helping the district achieve its strategic objectives, each school should identify site-specific manifestations of any district objective which is relevant and appropriate at that site. To focus on the highest priorities and to prevent overextension, only two or three school objectives should be set.

School objectives should always be consistent with the district's strategic plan. Since school staff will be expected to help implement the district's strategies, some school objectives should be directly related to the district's objectives. For example, a district might set a strategic objective "to have all students learn essential knowledge and skills in reading, writing, mathematics, science, and social science prior to high school graduation". A complementary elementary school objective might be "to have all students learn the essential knowledge and skills necessary for success at the middle school". Setting complementary school and district objectives is an important means of preventing overextension of staff. It is also an important way to assure a school's change effort is aligned with the district's.

Once a school's objectives are identified, tactics should be established to achieve those objectives. In a site plan, tactics are analogous to strategies in the district plan. They are long-term means of achieving objectives. The same cautions concerning overextension are relevant here. Tactics are the real determinants of work load. To avoid overextension, the planning team should only set the number of tactics necessary to achieve the school's objectives.

Finally, <u>action plans</u> will need to be developed for each of the tactics. As in the district's strategic plan, action plans are subdivisions of a tactic. Each action plan includes a specific result as well as a series of steps necessary to achieve that result. The outcome of implementing all the action plans is to fully implement each tactic.

Together, the components of a school/site plan define the long-term direction for the school. School/Site plans include the district's belief statement, as well as the school's own mission, internal analysis, external analysis, objectives, tactics, and action plans. When developed within the context of the district's strategic plan, school/site plans assure that each school's direction is consistent with the strategic direction of the district.

The Process for Developing School/Site Plans

The process for developing school/site plans is similar to that used for developing the district's strategic plan. The following steps are necessary:

1. Set the stage
2. Choose the planning team
3. Gather information
4. Hold first planning team session
5. Communicate results of first planning team session
6. Develop action plans
7. Hold second planning team session
8. Approve school/site plan
9. Organize for implementation
10. Conduct quarterly reviews of progress
11. Undertake annual updates

The first step in the process, setting the stage for developing the school/site plan, includes receiving authorization to proceed. Authorization typically comes from the superintendent with the knowledge and consent of the board. Developing school/site plans without proper authorization can be risky for a principal. When school/site plans are developed without authorization, those plans can be scuttled on a moment's notice at the whim of the superintendent or the board.

Setting the stage also involves clearly communicating to everyone in the school community why a school/site plan is being created; what the plan is designed to do; who will be on the planning team; and when the planning will take place. This communication keeps everyone informed and reduces suspicion, which often arises when something "new" is being initiated.

The second step in the process is selecting the school's planning team. The planning team is the primary work group for developing the school/site plan. Although it should be created in a manner similar to the district's strategic planning team, it should be a microcosm of the school rather than the district. The principal should be on the team, as should other building administrators. Teachers from different subject areas and grade levels, student services personnel, classified staff, and parents should also be tapped. Balance is very important. The desired outcome is to have a representative team.

There is one major qualification for planning team membership: Every group member must be a person of good will who cares about the success of the entire school. Planning team members should be concerned about the "common good," rather than a "special interest." The principal and the administrative staff usually select the team, but woe to the principal who stacks a team with "his or her people." If this is done, the entire process will lack credibility and be flawed from the beginning.

The third step in the process is to assemble background information for the planning team. This information should provide a "snapshot" of the school. It should include data concerning student performance, curriculum, personnel, budget, staff evaluation, and staff development programs at that school. Perhaps the most important information included is the district's strategic plan. The desired outcome is to provide members of the planning team with the information needed to make decisions without overwhelming them. It is important to avoid "analysis paralysis."

The background information is crucial to the success of the planning process. It provides the context necessary to make informed decisions. If this step is done well, people will have the common factual base necessary to make reasonable choices. They will also understand the district's strategic plan which will provide the guidance necessary to develop appropriate school/site plans. The background should be assembled in a notebook and sent to the planning team seven to ten days before the next step in the process: the first planning session.

The first planning session is the most critical step in the process. At the first planning session, the planning team will develop a draft of everything in the school/site plan except the action plans. Under the direction of a trained facilitator, the team will accomplish the following agenda:

Agenda: First Planning Session
1. Review the district's strategic plan
2. Discuss the district's beliefs
3. Develop the school's mission statement
4. Internal analysis for the school
5. External analysis for the school
6. Identify critical issues for the school
7. Identify school objectives
8. Establish tactics

As is true for the strategic plan, the planning team should make decisions by consensus. There should be no votes.

Because there is much less time spent on beliefs and because parameters are often not included, school/site planning sessions do not take as long as the first planning session for the strategic plan. Typically, eighteen to twenty-two hours will be sufficient to complete the agenda.

The next step is to communicate results of the first planning session throughout the school community. This step has two purposes: to inform all the school's constituents of progress to date, and to solicit volunteers for the action planning teams.

The next step is to develop action plans for each of the school's tactics. An action planning team will be created for each tactic. The charge of these teams is to develop the action plans necessary to fully implement the tactic. Members of the action teams should understand operational realities of the school. They should know how things get done. The action teams must honor the tactic as it is written. They do not have the right to amend or reject the tactic. As is true with the district's strategic plan, the action planning phase is the most time-consuming. Typically, three to four months are necessary.

Once action plans are completed, the second planning session is held. The purpose of this session is for the planning team to review the action plans and ensure that the action plans are consistent with the intent of the tactics.

There are two other purposes of the second planning session. First, the planning team should discuss an implementation schedule. Since it will be impossible to implement every action plan in the first year, some action plans will have to be held in abeyance for at least one year. The planning team can advise the principal as to which plans are most important to implement the first year. This is critically important in preventing overextension in pursuit of too many new initiatives.

Second, the planning team should review the school's preliminary mission, objectives, and tactics to see if any modifications are necessary. This is a check against inappropriate work at the first planning session. The action planning phase provides an opportunity to assess feedback concerning the components of the school/site plan. If changes are necessary, they can be made at the second planning session.

Next is the approval step. This is different than for the district's strategic plan. Usually, a school/site plan is approved by the principal's immediate supervisor. In many districts, this is the superintendent. In larger districts, it may be another central office administrator. Frequently, school/site plans are shared with the board of education, but formal board approval is rare.

There is a tendency to end the process here. However, this is dangerous. A planner's chief responsibility is not to get a plan approved; it is to ensure a plan can be implemented. Hence, the next step in the process is to carefully organize for implementation. This involves two steps. First, the plan should be written and distributed to the entire school staff as well as throughout the school's community. This step will inform everyone of the school's future direction, and it will help hold people accountable for implementation. Second, administrative responsibility should be assigned for every action plan which is to be implemented in the first year. If action plans are not part of an administrator's assigned responsibilities, they are often overlooked. The press of events in the normal school day frequently squeezes out new initiatives.

The next step in the process is to regularly assess progress implementing the plan. Quarterly reviews of progress on the action plans should be made by the administrative staff. These reviews help identify implementation problems early, as well as allow for justifiable mid-course corrections.

The final step is the annual update. The update is an opportunity to update and adjust the school's plan. To assure school plans are aligned with the district's, the school's update should follow the update of the district's strategic plan.

A great deal of creative energy is released during the development of school/site plans. When this creativity is aligned with the district's strategic plan, school/site plans become a powerful driving force for improving the entire school system as well as the individual school.

Summary

To ensure common direction in a school system, it is necessary to develop both strategic and school/site plans. School/Site plans developed without a district-wide strategic plan lack common focus. In a single district, they typically head in different directions with no means of holding anyone accountable for unspecified results.

Furthermore, a district-wide strategic plan that is not accompanied by school/site plans tends to be overly centralized. Too few people have been directly involved in the planning, and few people feel the sense of ownership that is crucial to successful implementation.

Combining the development of a district-wide strategic plan with complementary school/site plans is the key to transformation in a school district. As a centralizing force, the strategic plan defines common values, purpose, direction, and action over the long-term. As a decentralizing influence, school/site plans specify what actions will take place at individual schools. If developed within the context of the strategic plan, school/site plans will be consistent with as well as actively contribute to achievement of that strategic plan. Together, strategic and school/site plans balance the need for common direction with the desire for school autonomy.

Appendix 1

■

Groups: The Roles People Play

GROUPS — THE ROLES PEOPLE PLAY*

GROUP BLOCKING ROLES

The Aggressor
- Deflates status of others in group
- Disagrees with others aggressively
- Criticizes others in group

The Blocker
- Stubbornly disagrees and rejects others' views
- Cites unrelated personal experiences
- Returns to topics already resolved

The Withdrawer
- Will not participate
- Is a "wool gatherer"
- Carries on private conversations within group
- Is a self-appointed taker of notes

The Recognition Seeker
- Tries to show his importance through boasting and excessive talking
- Is overly conscious of his status

The Topic Jumper
- Continually changes the subject

The Dominator
- Tries to take over the meeting
- Tries to assert authority
- Tries to manipulate group

*Adapted from materials developed by the *American Management Association*

The Special Interest Pleader
- Uses the group's time to draw attention to his or her own concerns

The Playboy
- Wastes the group's time in showing off, telling funny stories, and the like
- Acts with nonchalance or cynicism

The Self-Confessor
- Talks irrelevantly about his own feelings and insights

The Devil's Advocate
- When he or she is more devil than advocate

GROUP BUILDING ROLES

The Initiator
- Suggests new or different ideas for discussion
- Proposes new or different approaches to problems

The Opinion Giver
- States pertinent beliefs about what the group is considering and others' suggestions

The Elaborator
- Elaborates or builds on suggestions made by others

The Clarifier
- Gives relevant examples
- Offers rationales
- Probes for meaning and understanding of matters under discussion
- Restates problems

The Tester
- Raises questions to "test out" whether the group is ready to come to a decision

The Summarizer
- Tries to pull together or reviews the discussion content

GROUP MAINTENANCE ROLES

The Tension Reliever
- Uses humor at appropriate times to draw off negative feelings
- Calls for a break at appropriate times

The Compromiser
- Does not stick stubbornly to his or her point of view, but is willing to yield when necessary for the progress of group

The Harmonizer
- Mediates differences of opinion
- Reconciles points of view

The Encourager
- Praises and supports others in their contributions
- Is friendly and encouraging

The Gate Keeper
- Keeps communications open
- Creates opportunities to encourage participation by others

Appendix 2

■ ■

A Sample Strategic Plan

BELIEFS

(Proposed as the district's fundamental convictions, values, and character.)

We believe that...

- Each individual has unique capabilities to learn.

- The protection and care of children are the priorities of any community.

- All people possess absolute universal human rights.

- Everyone deserves to be treated with respect.

- A community must have a moral foundation in order to thrive.

- Everyone has the right to the unrestricted pursuit of learning to the fullest of his/her capability.

- A community is only as strong as the contributions of its members toward the common good.

- Excellence is attainable by al.

- Challenging life experiences lead to personal growth.

- All people have the right to live in a safe, orderly environment.

- A healthy society is free of racism.

- Recognizing as well as honoring human diversity enriches the individual and the community.

- Human life has immeasurable value.

- All people have the resonsibility of protecting the natural environment.

- Higher expectations yield higher achievement.

- Public education is essential tot he survival of a free society.

MISSION

(Proposed as the unique purpose for which the school district exists and the specific function it performs.)

The mission of the XYZ School System, as the unifying force of our unique, diverse community, is to guarantee that each learner develops individual potential and becomes a contributing citizen through an educational system characterized by safe, nurturing environments; student-centered, creative learning; and an active, collaborating community.

OBJECTIVES

(Proposed as the desired and measurable end results for the district.)

The objectives of the XYZ School System are that...

- 100% of XYZ School System students will master all of the objectives of our core curriculum;

- 100% of XYZ School System students will be among the top 10% of their peers as measured by any validated international assessment;

- All XYZ School System students will be self-sustaining members of society.

- 100% of XYZ School System graduates will enter post-secondary eduction unconditionally or will successfully engage in a career of choice.

PARAMETERS

(Proposed as the established guidelines within which the district will accomplish its mission.)

- We will do nothing that is not based on the best interest of the student.
- We will offer only those courses, programs, or activities that are consistent with a PreK-12 instructional program.
- We will not tolerate racism or any other form of discrimination.
- We will never compromise quality.
- We will not accept failure.

STRATEGIES

(Proposed as the means of accomplishing the district's objectives.)

- We will design and implement a curriculum emphasizing the integration of academi and life skills that ensures the success of every student.
- We will guarantee the effectiveness of administrative and instructional staffs.
- We will achieve full family participation to accomplish our mission and objectives.
- We will achieve open communication among all participants in a student's education.
- We will ensure that the XYZ School System is a safe and orderly environment.

- We will achieve racial harmony throughout the school system.

- We will achieve community support and acquire resources essential to advance the success of each student.

- We will create student-centered learning environments.

Appendix 3

■ ■ ■

Mutual Commitments & Expectations

MUTUAL COMMITMENTS & EXPECTATIONS

I WILL DO THIS:		SO THAT:	MY SPECIFIC COMMITMENTS ARE:	STRATEGIC PLAN	THE SYSTEM SUPPORT REQUIRED IS:
• Direct/Immediate responsibilities		Results must be: •Consistent with context of Beliefs, Mission, Parameters, Objectives, and Strategies •Measurable, demonstrable, or observable •Direct immediate consequence(s) •Commensurate with: *decision-making prerogative *resources	• Specific measures in terms of time, money, quality, and/or quantity for each result • Specific demonstration of results (cause and effect) • Observable indicators of specific results.	• Reference to applicable strategies and action plans	• Expression of the whole system's commitment of energy and resources to expectations
Verb (2)	Noun (1)				
Relationships	Domain				

© 2000 THE CAMBRIDGE GROUP

127

MUTUAL COMMITMENTS & EXPECTATIONS

I WILL DO THIS:	SO THAT:	MY SPECIFIC COMMITMENTS ARE:	STRATEGIC PLAN	THE SYSTEM SUPPORT REQUIRED IS:
• Answers the question: What am I accountable for achieving? • Described as either: a. job components b. responsibility areas; or c. performance areas. • Start by listing *nouns* or *noun/adjective* combinations (DOMAIN) • After *nouns* are listed, select the *verb* which best describes the relationship to that domain. Don't use "wimpy verbs." • Identify 2-3 job components as key performance areas that are especially important this year.	• Answers the question: Why am I accountable for this? • Format: I will do this so that... • You may have more than one reason why you are accountable for a job component. • State the next, direct, immediate consequence(s). • Should be within your control: commensurate with your *decision-making prerogative, plus *resources • Often, rationale is found within Beliefs, Mission, Parameters, Objectives, and Strategies. • If this column is done correctly, the performance expectation for column 3 is usually implied.	• Answers the question: How well? How many? By when? At what cost? • State the expectation for your own performance this coming year. • Get at least 2 of the following in each performance expectation: a. time b. money c. quality d. quantity • These should be observable indicators of specific results • State at least one performance expectation for each reason "why" in the second column. • Often performance expectations are implied or stated explicitly for action plans scheduled to be implemented this coming year.	Direct Reference to specific strategies and action plans scheduled to be implemented this year.	• Answers the question: What type of support do I need from the system to meet or exceed my performance expectations this year. • May be written as specifically as necessary. • Could include: *Policy *Staff *Funding *Data *Evaluation *Equipment/ materials *Projects

NOTE: There are no "hows" on this form!

MUTUAL COMMITMENTS & EXPECTATIONS SAMPLE FORM

I WILL DO THIS:	SO THAT:	MY SPECIFIC COMMITMENTS ARE:	STRATEGIC PLAN	THE SYSTEM SUPPORT REQUIRED IS:

MUTUAL COMMITMENTS & EXPECTATIONS

I WILL DO THIS:	SO THAT:	MY SPECIFIC COMMITMENTS ARE:	STRATEGIC PLAN	THE SYSTEM SUPPORT REQUIRED IS:
1. Direct Biannually Bus Evacuation Drill	1a. Drivers will know what to do in the event of an emergency. 1b. Students will know what to do in the event of an emergency. 1c. State guidelines will be followed.	• Evacuation drills will be completed by all bus drivers as quickly as possible, but not more than 90 seconds with 90% accuracy. • All drivers will follow the State guidelines for school evacuation drills by having drills twice a year, October and February, with 95% accuracy.	II-4	• Management of Contract Company will be responsible for all Maintenance. • Support of Trans. Department. • Support of Handicapped Student Trans. Office.
2. Conduct Quarterly Bus Inspections	2a. Buses will be safe and meet the Sate Guidelines for School bus safety. 2b. Buses will be checked monthly for items that need to be repaired. 2c. Buses will not operate if they are not safe and don't meet State Guidelines.	• State inspector will inspect all Contract buses once a year with 99% accuracy. • The Coordinator for the Birmingham City Schools will inspect all contract buses four times a year for any safety violations according to State Guidelines with 90% accuracy.	II-5	• The State Department of Education will set the guidelines for transportation. • Support of Coordinator of Sp. Ed. Trans. • Support of Contract Management for all maintenance violations.
3. Coordinate Sp. Ed. Transportation with Contract Bus Company	3a. Contract buses will transport Sp. Ed. Students daily to an from school. 3b. Contact company will follow all terms of the contract. 3c. Contract Company will follow all guidelines set by the State Department of Education.	• Contract Company will receive payments monthly according to the terms of the contract with 99% accuracy. • Payment will be calculated at the end of every month at the rate 365 students per day. Overages will only be paid if there are over 365 transported per day.	II-1	• Support of Trans. Department. • Support of Handicapped Student Trans. • Support of Contract Management for all route information for payment. • Support of Board of Education.

MUTUAL COMMITMENTS & EXPECTATIONS

I WILL DO THIS:	SO THAT:	MY SPECIFIC COMMITMENTS ARE:	STRATEGIC PLAN	THE SYSTEM SUPPORT REQUIRED IS:
4. Direct Transportation for Special Education Students that qualify	4a. Special Education students will receive door to door service. 4b. Students will not ride on Contract buses longer than on-hour one way. 4c. Students will go to a school in their area if there is a program for that child. If a program is not in child's area, the child will be transported by Contract Company.	• Students will be transported from the students house 100% of the time. • Students will not ride bus longer than an hour to or from school 90% of the time. • Students will go to a school where a program can be provided for the child needs with 95% accuracy. • Students will be transported outside of their area for program needs with 99% accuracy.	II-1	• Support of Transportation Department. • Support of Handicapped Student Trans. • Support of Contract Management for all pick-ups and deliveries • Support of Board of Education
5. Direct parental reimbursement for parents that transport their own Special Ed. Children to school. (Usually out of the child's school zone.)	5a. Parents will be reimbursed for the miles transporting their child to and from school. 5b. Parents who transport their children every day and will be responsible for their child's safety. 5c. Parent will receive payment twice a year.	• Parents transporting their children will receive $.25 a mile or a minimum or $1.00 a day with 95% accuracy. • Parents will receive payment based on the days the child comes to school with 99% accuracy.	II-1	• Support of Transportation Department. • Support of Handicapped Student Trans. • Support of Contract Management • Support of Board of Education • Teacher, Parent and School support.
6. Directly oversee the terms of the Contract for the Contract Company for the Birmingham School System.	6a. Monitoring of the Contract Company. 6b. Providing support for the Contract Company that they will need. 6c. Utilized the resources provided to operate the Transportation for the Handicapped.	• The Contract Company will follow the terms of the contract with 100% accuracy. • The Transportation Dept. will provide 100% of the support to help make sure that all of the operations run smooth with 95% accuracy.	II-1	• Support of Transportation Department. • Support of Handicapped Student Trans. • Support of Contract Management • Support of Board of Education • Teacher, Parent and School support.

MUTUAL COMMITMENTS & EXPECTATIONS

I WILL DO THIS:	SO THAT:	MY SPECIFIC COMMITMENTS ARE:	STRATEGIC PLAN	THE SYSTEM SUPPORT REQUIRED IS:
7. Providing vital student information for the contract company.	7a. Student information will be provided on every child that receives Transportation Services. 7b. Parents will notify the Transportation Department when student information changes. 7c. Teachers will inform transportation office of any change of student information.	• The Transportation Department will provide the Contract Company with student information in August with 95% accuracy. • Updated information will be provided when available by the Transportation Dept. with 90% accuracy.	II-1	• Support of Transportation Department. • Support of Handicapped Student Trans. • Support of Contract Management • Support of Board of Education • Teacher, Parent and School support.
8. Coordinate Behavioral Problems between the School, Teacher, Parent or Contract Company.	8a. Teachers will work with Principal and Contact Company to solve problems that occur on the bus. 8b. Principal will work with Trans. Dept. and Contract Company to solve bus problems. 8c. Contact Company will work with Trans. Dept. and schools to solve any bus problems.	• The Contract Company will solve 90% of the bus behavioral problems at the local school level. • The Contract Company will work with the parents, attendants teachers and principals when needed to solve problems concerning the bus with 95% accuracy.	II-1	• Support of Transportation Department. • Support of Handicapped Student Trans. • Support of Contract Management • Support of Board of Education • Teacher, Parent and School support.
9. Direct monthly safety meetings with STS for the drivers and the attendances.	9a. Drivers will attend safety meetings once a month. 9b. Attendances will attends a safety meeting once a month. 9c. Drivers and attendants will know how to perform safety procedures when needed.	• All drivers will attend one safety meeting a month as required by Contract Management. • All attendances will attend one safety meeting a month as required by Contract Management.	II-5	• Support of Transportation Department. • Support of Handicapped Student Trans. • Contract Management Support • Contract Management will supervise drivers and attendants with assistance of the Board of Ed.

MUTUAL COMMITMENTS & EXPECTATIONS

I WILL DO THIS:	SO THAT:	MY SPECIFIC COMMITMENTS ARE:	STRATEGIC PLAN	THE SYSTEM SUPPORT REQUIRED IS:
10. Monitor monthly trip sheets for every route on every bus that transports Special Ed. Students to a Birmingham City School.	10a. Collecting the trip sheets each week will determine how Contract Company will receive payment each week. 10b. Contract Company will only get paid for the students that ride the bus. 10c. Drivers will mark only those students that ride the bus to and from school.	• Contact Company will have every bus driver keep a trip sheet one very child that rides the bus 100% of the time. • Contact Company will keep a route sheet on every bus for every child with 100% accuracy.	II-2	• Support of Transportation Department. • Support of Handicapped Student Trans. • Contract Management Support • Contract Management will supervise drivers and attendants with assistance of the Board of Ed.
11. Bus Drivers will maintain a good safe school bus environment. Contract Company will supervise drivers and bus maintenance with the assistance of the Board of Ed.	11a. Drivers will be responsible for the students on his or her bus. 11b. Students must follow all rules set by the Contact Company and the Board. 11c. The bus attendants will help students obey all rules on the bus. 11d. The bus attendants will help drivers maintain order while the bus is in motion.	• The bus drivers will be responsible for every one on their bus 100% of the time. • Students will obey rules for riding the bus with 90% accuracy. The Attendants will help monitor the students as they travel back and forth to school 100% of the time.	II-5	• Support of Transportation Department. • Support of Handicapped Student Trans. • Contract Management Support • Contract Management will supervise drivers and attendants with assistance of the Board of Ed.
12. Drivers will Pre-Trip buses before the bus is moved (morning and afternoon)	12a. Driver will Pre-Trip bus every day. This will cut down on breakdowns. 12b. Drivers will notify maintenance of any problem daily. 12c. Maintenance will make repairs quickly so buses will return to service quickly.	• Drivers will pre-trip their buses twice daily with 100% accuracy (morning and afternoon). • The service department will have the bus back in service the very next day 90% of the time. • Sub buses will be used when repairs can't be made within the one-day time frame 10% of the time.	II-5	• Support of Transportation Department. • Support of Handicapped Student Trans. • Contract Management Support • Contract Management will supervise drivers and attendants with assistance of the Board of Ed.

Appendix 4

■ ■ ■ ■

Total-Gain Decision Making

TOTAL-GAIN
DECISION-MAKING

The decision-making method employed by the Action Teams is critical to the strategic planning activity for at least two reasons. First, the credibility of the entire planning process is at risk, so to speak. The slightest infraction of the principles of full participation and shared decision making, however understood by those involved, can not only destroy the effectiveness of an Action Team, but it can also seriously damage the organization's strategic planning effort. Therefore, extreme care must be taken to employ a decision-making process(es) beyond reproach. Second, the quality of the plans is at stake. Experience proves again and again that some popular management approaches to decisions (notably, any of the permutations of Machiavellian manipulation) are obviously counterproductive. Since they represent one, usually biased, point of view, the plans themselves are typically exercises in resistance to change. Furthermore, no plan, regardless of how good it is, that is developed in exclusion can expect to be inclusive in implementation.

But participation in decision-making does not guarantee either credibility or quality. Even if the organization is sincerely committed to the full involvement of all concerned persons, sometimes it is difficult to escape the lingering influence of political and corporate systems that by their very nature are adverse to both participation and transformation. So most attempts of team or group decision-making do not live up to their promise because they are stymied by either "democratic" processes or something called "consensus." Both are fundamentally flawed and sure to end in disappointment.

THE DEMOCRATIC PROCESS

Democratic decision-making is predicated on the twin axioms of political democracy: majority rule and voting. The first means that there will always be winners and losers; the second, that nothing is ever finally resolved. Recently, something buzz-worded "win-win" has captured the popular fancy as a happy way of overcoming the inevitable conflict in democratic processes. However, not only is this a logical impossibility, it also presupposes that decision-making is a competitive exercise, and that the group, team, and organization is permanently divided and contrary.

Ouchi's Theory Z definition

"Consensus" decision-making as understood and practiced by most organizations today derives from Ouchi's Theory Z definition: Consensus has been reached when participants can say:

"I believe that you understand my point of view."

"I believe that I understand your point of view."

"Whether or not I prefer this idea or concept I will support it because it was

reached openly and fairly."

"I can live with this decision."

Since that decree over thirty years ago, all kinds of "consensus" related terms and methodologies have been concocted and prescribed by a host of management gurus. But the consensus seems to be that "consensus" is both a rational process of negotiating a settlement and the resulting decision. That is to say, it is at once both means and end. It is "built" as well as "achieved." But no matter what definitions or techniques are used, in practice (and, likely, in philosophy since both originate in the context of the corporation), "consensus" is nothing more than a non-voting version of the democratic process in which the real losers are conned to peacefully acquiesce to the will of the majority. They do so because they have been peremptorily

138

pledged to support an artificial process over their own convictions. So any "consensus" is, in fact, artificial and lacking the emotional support necessary for its complete realization. The venacular of the day declares the truth: "majority consensus" (U.S. Congress); "significant consensus" (state education reform legislation); "quasi-consensus" (directive from state department of education). Whatever consensus might be, surely, it has nothing to do with contemporary definitions.

TOTAL-GAIN DECISION-MAKING

The only approach that guarantees both the credibility and quality of participative decision-making has no popular cachet. And, unfortunately, not much of a following. Even so, decision-making is effective only to the degree that groups achieve, for lack of a better term, "total-gain agreement." That is to say, decision-making in which 100% of the participants are satisfied that the decision reached represents a benefit or advantage to them that they could not have achieved without the involvement of the group. In other words, everyone experiences "gain" that would be impossible without the dynamics and contributions of the group.

"Total-gain" decision-making requires a discipline beyond process or methodology. It requires constant adherence by all participants to certain principles. These commitments must be made before decision-making begins, and must be religiously honored:

- All decisions will be consistent with the organization's stated beliefs.
- All decisions will be made in the context of the organization's stated mission and strategic objectives.
- All decisions will be made in the best interest of the student.
- All decisions will follow the golden rule.
- Participation will be commensurate with actual knowledge and/or experience.
- Each participant will always tell the truth.

139

- A final decision does not mean an end to conversation, review, and reconsideration.

Far more than cliché or methodology, this kind of decision-making essentially reflects a mature organizational culture that, although rare, is certainly possible. But it is achieved only when all participants are dedicated to a cause that transcends themselves.

ESSAYS ON STRATEGY

✤

EXCERPTS FROM

THE STRATEGIC PLANNER FOR EDUCATION

As a special feature of this edition, we have included
several essays on strategy. These were taken from a column
titled, "Notes from the Publisher," that first appeared in
The Strategic Planner for Education, an educational journal
dedicated to the creation of new systems of education.

~ I ~

Strategic Planning Revisited

❧

Strategic Planning, as the name implies, is the only kind of planning that even purports to deal with true strategic issues. But the problem is, throughout North America, in business as well as the public sector, hordes of well intentioned people are rushing headlong into a general confusion they call strategic planning.

The most superficial of these approaches are the ones based on the assumption that strategic planning is merely a methodology; that is, a process and/or discipline with certain prescribed components which, no matter how defined or developed, constitute a plan. Even the most precise terminology within the most technically accurate methodology will not produce a strategic plan unless the issues dealt with are, in fact, strategic. Strategic issues of necessity deal with who the organization is, why it exists, and usually what it hopes to achieve by way of measurable results. The how is left to operational planning within the strategic context.

The problem is that a dramatic coincidence of historical velocity and the natural life cycles of most industrialite organizations has forced a continuing redefinition of these strategic issues. Now, it is fairly obvious that anything written or practiced in strategic planning prior to 1986 is itself obsolete. And anything after that date that does not see strategic issues in a new reality is already obsolete.

Specifically, in the late 40s, 50s and 60s, strategic planning typically and properly was utilized in de novo situations—start-up enterprises without precedent, based on assumptions about the potential market or actual demand. But by the 1970s, owing to the sterility of financiers, this kind of planning had degenerated into the development of formulaic "business plans."

In that same decade, strategic planning was properly applied to change issues—specifically, Level I change issues. This means change within a system described as "improvement," "restructuring," "reforming"; but it remained the same system. It is regrettable to note that most of today's so-called strategic planning still uses the vocabulary and, I suppose, the concepts of Level I change.

Since 1986, strategic issues have been redefined in terms of Level II change, and that demands planning that results in creating something other than the original system. The questions of "who" and "why" and "what" are still valid, but the results are in a new language and constitute a complete metamorphosis of the planning organization. New in kind replaces new in time.

I doubt that all the current confusion over planning will do any harm to real strategic planning. But, sadly, the confusion will assuredly destroy many organizations and systems. Even sadder, they won't realize what happened. ❖

~ II ~

Land, Ho! - part one

❧

In a great sea-change like this, there are naturally many currents and cross-currents, the gales are sudden and treacherous; a certain course is difficult to set and maintain. Ships founder and sink; some hit the sand.

No wonder why we as facilitators are asked so often to make some sense of the confusing currents in education. This year, like never before, with almost every presentation, I am asked the same desperate question by someone: "How do Strategic Planning, Total Quality Management, Management by Objectives/ Results, Participatory Management, Outcomes-Based Education, Effective Schools, School Improvement, *et cetera* all fit together? Or do they?" Good questions. So let's attempt to sort these things out.

The first obstacle we have to get through is the totally erroneous assumption that these terms all belong to the same logical category and can thus be directly compared and contrasted with one other or, in cases of preference, substituted for each other. Actually, what we have here are two distinct categories of items: First, there are those that deal with objective matters; that is enterprises that are intrinsic and unique to the business at hand and cannot be transferred to another except by use of analogy. For example, "The soul of the company is its bottom line," versus "The bottom line of this church is souls." Tight-rope walkers and acrobats debate the moral implications of safety nets; governments declare safety nets a moral imperative.

Then there are the subjective matters; that is values and philosophies that are, in fact, subject-centered and which provide both the context for establishing the objective matters to be pursued as well as the methodologies involved in application and realizations of various enterprises toward whatever end. For example, once a person chooses a career as a coach (subjective), he/she is immediately faced with myriad possibilities (objective) in the world of sports. Paradoxically enough, I think most people and organizations are in trouble because they concentrate most of their effort on that which is objective and completely ignore the subjective.

All of which, happily, brings us back to the subject at hand—the confusion in the sea of education. Quite simply, I would consider Outcome-Based Education, Effective Schools, and School Improvement activities and others of their kind to be objective matters—even moreso than concepts like "cooperative learning" and "whole languages." These somewhat programmatic practices are intrinsic to the business of education; they do not transfer to other businesses. In fact, they are specific to existing systems of education in North America, and evidently presuppose the continuation of these systems *ad infinitum*. To their credit, however, the advocates of these programs recognize the need for some kind of subjective context; hence, they lately turned to planning activity or management philosophy as a starting place.

I do not think it possible for strategic planning facilitators to champion my particular expression of any objective matter. If I, as a facilitator, do that, then my subjectivity has destroyed my objectivity and the client's emphasis on objectivity will preclude any subjectivity whatsoever. I don't see how strategic planning can proceed under those circumstances, and that explains why so many are lost at sea. ❖

~ III ~

Land, Ho! ~ part two

❧

If objective matters are, by their nature, precisely denied even to the point of enforcement, subjective matters, by their nature, are susceptible to interpretation, misunderstanding and confusion. They are constituted of principle, not doctrine; they are realized through exercise, not application.

For example, Management By Objectives, a philosophy from the administrative school of classical management, was and is founded on a sound principle: that is, that desired end results should be the validation of all organized activity. With that intense concentration on outcomes, anything which does not measurably contribute to specific objectives, also measurable, is abandoned. But rigid application rather than reasonable exercise turned principle into doctrine, and eventually management by objectives resulted in the fragmentation of both jobs and organizations and in the practice of justifying means by ends—both disastrous to the organization. But the fundamental idea is still a good one.

The same thing seems to be happening to something new called Total Quality Management. It is very telling that the originators of the basic concept—the principle—never used the new popular phrase to describe it, and even now the most ardent advocates and practitioners cannot say for sure what the adjective "total" modifies—quality or management. The idea springs from the Operational Research Models of the scientific management schools—using mathematical analysis to calibrate the functioning parts of an integrated system toward full efficiency. It's really hard to argue with that concept. And what of the idea of quality, particularly as defined by customers? Great idea. And what about the "participatory" approach to designing total systems to exceed customer expectations? Again, superlative idea. But, unfortunately, application of principle as rigid authority will (1) sacrifice effectiveness to efficiency (2) obscure

147

results with process and (3) substitute organizational conditions, positive or negative, for actual individual accountability. Even worse is the unjustifiable expectation that TQM can lead to the radical transformation of organizations, which is tantamount to the creation of new ones, rather than managing the improvement, even the perfection, of existing organizations. So far, no one has been able to explain how quantitative improvements translates into qualitative gains. This paradoxically is one instance in which customer expectation cannot be met, much less exceeded.

The ultimate subjective matter is probably strategic planning. The concept, over 6,000 years old in a military context, was recast in a broader and more qualitative organizational context as the scientific management movement developed at mid-century. Ultimate because, if properly understood, it would deal with the very identity of the organization—the who, why, and what of its being. And, if properly exercised, would continually create the organization toward extraordinary purpose. ❖

~ IV ~

A CURRENT QUANDARY

❧

I don't know which is worse: the transmogrification of management into something pretentiously termed "leadership" or the relegation of strategic planning to management. Both mistakes result in unmitigated disaster. Just as a reminder, *strategos* means "to lead." To make it merely a scientific technique is to rob it of its inherent power to leverage an entire organization into a new reality, and that is what leading is all about.

Consider this. If strategic planning is true to its name, it will partake of the critical attributes of leaders. I believe that there are universal characteristics of leaders, and that these characteristics are derived from the group allowing itself to be led rather than developed by objectified training into a commodity to be bought and sold in the marketplace. Quite simply, leading is not a matter of the application of skills; it is not even a matter of becoming; it is a matter of being.

Four characteristics will suffice to make the point. And most of these have much to do with current notions of "leadership." First, leaders see things that ordinary people have not seen yet. Many people these days are much enamored of "vision"—by popular practice a cotton-candyish concoction of fond wish and silliness—on a shtick. If this is the only dimension we ascribe to sight then we are indeed hopelessly lost. The seeing of future things is the job of prophets; being out front is the job of scouts. Sure, leaders possess instinctive foresight, but equally valuable is their hindsight and insight. By hindsight I mean their passionate reverence for the history, culture, traditions, and values that made them leaders; and by insight I mean their empathetic knowledge of who we are that calls us to be true to ourselves. This three-dimensional sight is also characteristic of real strategic planning.

Second, all leaders I know are committed to a cause that transcends themselves. This translates into two practical expressions: they are willing

149

to subordinate themselves to that cause, and they will attempt things that other people think bold, even reckless. The first expression is an issue of morality; leaders know that if something is not good, it cannot be better. The second expression is a matter of defining reality; leaders by nature constantly push the line separating the possible from the impossible. So it is with real strategic planning.

Third, all leaders live in risk. I say "in risk" rather than "at risk" because leaders never consider failure an option. The only thing they risk is success. The reason is so simple: leaders move strictly by principle—not precedent. Think about it—those who rely on precedent are followers—not leaders. True strategic planning, however, is always an act of creation and the result always unique, distinctive, one of a kind.

Fourth, all leaders exist in a state of grace. That is, they personify the value system of the group that chose to set them forth as the embodiment of who they are. Leaders are not assigned; they are not imposed; they are not hired; they cannot be imported—they are chosen. And those who choose them reserve the right to reject them if their own image of themselves is ever violated. A true strategic plan is also indigenous to the group: it is the full expression of that organization's value system rendered in terms of specific moral imperatives.

Now that I think about it, I do know which is worse. ❖

~ V ~

DEFENSIO PRO MEO OFFICIO

❧

Maybe I'm just having a bad season, but lately I'm feeling a bit like Nick Carroway—"So we beat on, boats against the current, borne back ceaselessly into the past."

I realize that we walk a fine line. On the one hand, we are facilitators, professionals dedicated to a craft, attempting to apply, as best we can, a rational technique to stimulate self-motivated transformation of our clients. On the other hand, all of us have an unyielding commitment to public education. First, as the basic requirement of a free society; and, second, as the best means of providing each person with the opportunity to develop fully his or her own genius. Everyone who reads this column is essentially a volunteer in this cause.

The mission of Cambridge, I trust, is the mission of us all: ...*to transform educational systems to achieve extraordinary purpose by inspiring and enabling people and their organizations to recreate themselves.* And I'm convinced that we have the clearest understanding of strategic planning and the most effective planning process and discipline available anywhere. But lately it has occurred to me, as I wander to and fro over the continent, that the fervent attitude of reform that dominated the intellectual, political, and academic landscape during the past decade is losing its zing. Everywhere I go, I am sensing disappointment, resignation, and, now, even resistance. It is the resistance that bothers me most. The current is against transformation. Everywhere.

First, consider the federal government. It is a tragic farce of immense proportions. Everyday the public is barraged about the need for health care reform, welfare reform, crime control, employment, and housing. All the news is old. Evidently it has escaped the attention of our cynical federal lawmakers that education is the answer to all the other reforms. I submit that it is not enough merely to draft six so-called national goals—

151

vapid and irrelevant as they are—and walk away. Tell me I'm wrong: The federal government has essentially given up on public education. Placebos have replaced principle. And I know why. Kids don't vote.

Second, consider the states—the entities charged constitutionally with providing systems of education. I simply do not believe that you can find a more tangled mess on earth than the jury-rigged, Rube Goldberg machinery constructed by politicians, bureaucrats, and special interest groups. As far as I can tell, only one state, Utah, has even considered the possibility of creating systems that serve the best interests of students. Last year we tried to count all the special interest groups affecting state legislation and policies pertaining to education. While we still do not have a final tally, we did discover one despicable fact. There is no special interest group of, by, or for kids. I'm sorry folks. You can argue that one if you want, but you can only lose.

Third, consider the local situation. I'm beginning to think that in many cases, if any teaching and learning takes place at all it can only be explained by the persistent and powerful force of teaching and learning itself and the commitment of good people to a value they dare not lose. It is certainly not because these local systems are doing much even to aid and abet what is going on in the classroom. I know that the districts are plagued by the ills of their community—crime, drugs, poverty, racism—but, there are also the internal problems of incompetent, fractionalized boards, forsworn community groups, shrill administrators, and firebrand unions—all of whom are more and more blatantly sacrificing students to their own interests. I'm sorry, Pollyanna. It's time you faced the truth. The absolute worst thing that could happen to us as facilitators—or to strategic planning—is that we be used to any advantage other than the students'. ❖

~ VI ~

IMPLEMENTATION AND PLANNING

❧

All of us in the business of facilitating strategic planning have known for a long time that the most critical part of the exercise is the "implementation" of the plan. Technically, implementation is a part of neither the plan nor planning, but both gain their credibility only if the plan is successfully carried out. The surest way to destroy good faith and to replace it with frustration and cynicism is to develop a plan full of high resolve and exquisite detail and then have it relegated to the museum or morgue along with all the other ancient lifeless promises.

It is for that reason that the Cambridge system of planning was developed by back-formation. The first consideration was (and is) discovering and applying the very best means—be it format or form—to insure that whatever plans are developed can be actually realized. And I think it indisputable that our system does that better than any other planning methodology. But that is no longer enough.

Early on, we never presumed that we should deal with the question of whether the plan will be implemented. But now we do. I still believe that the issue ultimately is out of the purview of facilitation. However, since it is not the practicality but the practice of the plans that is the test of our credibility, it behooves us to assume an expanded role in, and obligation for implementation. It is not just a matter of business—it is a matter of conscience.

This is the precise situation: because of the effectiveness of our system, the skill of our facilitators, and the foresight and daring of the planning teams, we are creating plans for districts who do not have the capacity to realize their own strategies. This circumstance contains more potential for frustration and cynicism than simply shelving the plans. People will search for the pony for only so long before they quit believing in Santa.

Our only right response to this situation is to involve ourselves—as facilitators, not consultants—in the district's efforts to develop its own capacity. We have attempted to do this to some degree in our current implementation phase. In fact, as far as I know, we are the only planners who include any attempt at implementation in the basic planning system. However, our process, which relies primarily on developing mutual expectations and commitments, is based, I'm sorry to say, on the mistaken notions that adequate organizational capacities exist and that we are dealing with rational systems.

There are three aspects of capacity creation. First, there is the necessity after the strategic plan is accepted, to develop a full and clear concept of how the district will uniquely organize to accomplish its mission. Second, there must be established mutual expectations and commitments between the system and the individuals who are a part of it. Third, corresponding expectations and commitments must be established between the system and its components and, at the same time, among the components. Because each of these aspects presents a multiplicity of options and because each is subject to a broad spectrum of understanding and interpretation, it would be presumptuous of us as facilitators to recommend any specific solution, but we are derelict if we do not exact commitment and follow-through by the district. ❖

You Can't Roller Skate in a Buffalo Herd

❧

It now appears that our friend, the late departed Roger, was right all along. Oh, we hummed the tune well enough, but we did not understand the words. But, then, that's precisely the point, isn't it.

Context. It's all a matter of context. Without that, nothing makes any sense—precisely because nothing has any meaning without it.

Probably the greatest paradox of the rationalization of production by human organizations (management X philosophy) is the progressive obliteration of context by the relentless pursuit of perfection in the components which sooner or later become mere fragments. At some point, we forget why.

Take this simple test: exactly when does information become knowledge in your organization? Even more basic: when does data become information? If these questions cannot be answered with confidence, then chances are that at least one activity within the organization is meaningless. And if one activity is without meaning, so are all the others. That is the nature of context.

There are three ways to approach the matter of context: (1) ignore it, and move in all directions simultaneously, doing any and all things at once; (2) accept the context prescribed by precedent or external factors; or (3) create your own. Strategic planning is all about creating your own. Only, I'm afraid that sometimes we have not given the subject the attention or emphasis it must have.

For example, if we think that context is provided by the mission, or any other single factor, we have lost our own context. One-dimensional context is oxymoronic.

Everything on the planet, whether natural or artifactual, has four dimensions. (I conclude that after more than a half century of dedicated observation, so this is not an argument but a report.) Therefore, it stands to reason that organization, whether natural or artifactual, also has four dimensions.

Do not expect to see these dimensions. Because they are constantly interacting, they cannot be portrayed, in any way, as static. Any attempt to symbolize them could at best only approximate what the relationship among the dimensions was at one fleeting moment.

But we can understand them. The first dimension is the *common values* of the group of people who have agreed to organize themselves for a specific enterprise. These values are fundamental bedrock convictions held in common by all in the group. In our planning, we term these "beliefs." Since these are moral imperatives, we could also call them commitments.

The second dimension is the intent of the enterprise itself—the *mutual purpose* on which organization is based, if indeed it represents the group's highest aspiration. We term this "mission," as if it were an extraordinary undertaking of serious, even noble, resolve. And that is exactly what it must be.

The third dimension is *excess capacity*; that is, total wherewithal of the group organizing to be true to its own commitments and to realize its aspirations. There are at least three things that we must learn about the matter of capacity: (1) it is created, only within individual persons, (2) it is always created outside the context of the existing system, and (3) it always is excess.

The fourth dimension is *immediate action*. It's this simple: somebody—everybody—actually has to do something. But the action is more than merely the prerequisite to specific results. It is a constant. It is, in fact, both the testing and the creation of the organization's reality. Each person in the system must be able to act independently yet in concert.

Strategic planning, by its very nature, is ultimately the making of these dimensions. It's as simple as either getting all the buffaloes on skates or learning how to gallop real fast. ❖

~ VIII ~

A Code of Change

❧

I've been thinking a lot lately about change. Maybe it's because suddenly I have become a SOG (Slightly Older Guy); maybe it's because Jill is getting married this summer; or, most likely, it's because telephone company arbitrarily changed our area code. I think it was the phone folly that actually tipped me into an unusually pensive, sometime agitated, mood about the whole business of change. You see, I had lived with that area code all my life, grew up with it, thought it a part of my identity. Now it's gone.

The change was, in fact, unprecedented. Oh, there have been a rash of area code adjustments lately (I still can't remember if it's 312 or 708), but the inexplicable move from 205 to 334 represents unparalleled arrogance by the phone company (eminent domain attitude, I suspect), to say nothing of unparalleled yobbish bumbling (typical guaranteed-profit public utility mentality) and provincial government ditherings (a similar change was blocked by the courts in Washington). Harsh criticism, you say? Uncharacteristic of yours truly? Well, consider this: area code 334 at this time cannot be reached by some phones. In fact, many phones. There are 400,000 PBX systems in use today; 200,000 of them cannot recognize 334. So we have been rendered virtually an island, cut off from the communications mainland by a vast chasm of buffoonery. (We obviously were quite prescient when we named our firm Colonial.) Several major companies are filing suit; average customers are complaining like the dickens; the phone company says it's all going according to plan.

I think the whole affair, as insane as it is, provides an endless array of unbelievable case studies, and one or two object lessons. At least, it got me thinking very seriously about change. Actually, I've been trying to ease my mind by contemplating the words of a man whose life was change, Marcus Aurelius Antoninus: "The universe is change; our life is what our thoughts make of it."

Think about that. Marc's message is still loud and clear and he never even heard of an area code. I'm personally very connected to him—friends and family, as it were. If you listen, you can still hear him saying, in his true voice:

"Lend me your ears. A pox on the phone company and all their bastard offspring." What you must do is to learn from this folly. Look at it like this: there are four popular notions about change, and I'm telling you that they are false, so don't fall prey to them. Listen to me.

You've been led to believe that change is an *abstraction*. But it most assuredly is not so. It hits you every day in every part of your life. It is incidental, it is continual, it is pervasive. It does not lurk as if ready to pounce; it is essential to all things. It is as real as anything you can see, touch, or otherwise experience. It is you, yourself. Remember, Heraclitus observed almost five-hundred years ago that 'nothing endures but change.' And ask yourself this question, 'Where is Heraclitus now?'

You've also been told that change is *unnatural*. What can I say other than what I've already said, 'The universe is change'? I mean by that to say change is really desirable, possibly an innate human need—a craving, if you will. So, if people have any natural affinity to natural things, I would assume they would happily embrace, yes even vigorously pursue, change as the way of life. By the way, I must point out that the word that seems to attract most attention in our marketplaces is 'change' (that's *novus* to you).

You've also been counselled that change is *resistible*. My advice is that you check that advice quickly with my late friend Julius. You can run, but you can't hide. You can fight, but you can't win. You can importune, but you will find no sympathy. Change has been around much longer than you, and, I'm sorry to report, will be around much longer than you.

I do, however, have cheering news. You've also been told that change is *uncontrollable*. Pray don't believe that. Just remember two things: first, the simple fact is that, save for non man-made natural disasters, all the change that troubles us or challenges us in human affairs is made by humans themselves. Second, you don't have to put up with it if you didn't make it or if you don't like it. That's why I said, 'Our life is what our thoughts make of change.' Think passive, get ready to be pushed around. But think assertively, have a good life. So you see, there are only two ways to deal with change: you can create it, and you can control it yourself.

Sorry. Got to run. I hear Octavian is making rumbling noises again up north. Seems he wants to re-code my area.

Chiao bello, bambinos.

ALEXANDRIA

XV-III-XXXIV

I thank whatever gods may be for Marc. He just convinced me that we can rise above this area code madness. Our website is www.colonialcam-bridge.com. I'll talk to you there. ❖

~ IX ~

New Dimensions of Strategic Planning

❧

J ust about the time we begin to think that we have the business of strategic planning well in hand in terms of both understanding and application, just at the moment we are about to drift into the comfort of routine long since mastered—WHAM! The original, basic concept of strategic planning dramatically thrust itself upon us with the same, irresistible energy that has recreated systems for over five centuries. It's as if the idea continually regenerated itself. This year that vitality has been realized in at least three new dimensions.

First, the decline of the traditional corporation-model organization has been attended by a general system dysfunctionality. That means it is increasingly difficult to accomplish truly effective strategic planning, even with honest dedicated intent. The problem is the lack of capacity within these weakened systems—specifically, the unwillingness to deal with strategic issues and the inability to implement the plan. That's why from now on we will be concerned about much more than just the process and discipline of planning. In case you haven't noticed, our revised material greatly expands the application of strategic concepts to include "strategic thinking" as a necessary context and "strategic action" as the practical result of strategic planning. In our new video, which will be available early next year, these concepts will be given as much emphasis as the technicalities and methodologies of planning.

Second, the state (province)-based network that we began developing in 1986 through the International Planning Center for Education® continues to grow apace. This year we will welcome at least six new affiliates, the most in any single year since 1986-87. And the state (province) programs continue to increase their activities and influence, primarily through the efforts of their cadres of external facilitators. This dramatic expansion not only proves the wisdom of the decision to localize our delivery system, but it also attests to the increasing realization that strategic planning is neither fad nor luxury.

Third, there is all around us an entirely new phenomenon—one of incalculable proportions—with regard to the accelerated reformation of organizational systems. Specifically, it is now abundantly clear that the monolithic, monopolistic educational system—of, by, and for the industrial age—is well on its way to breaking apart. The parts, as they declare their identities and begin to discover their "niches" will, in the aggregate, constitute whatever new order(s) there is. For example: charter schools and specialized educational support enterprises (public or private). The significance for us is that each and every one of these entities will, sooner or later, require strategic thinking, strategic planning, and strategic action. This means that if we are to remain the premier planning group in North America and more importantly, if we are to serve the needs of the entire educational community, there are three significant changes that we must make. One, we must be willing ourselves to think beyond our own experiences, expectations, and comfort. Two, we must rise above any personal loyalties to existing artifacts. And, third, we must be flexible in our design and application of strategic concepts to the point of bringing a unique approach to every situation which, as never before, will be unique. All things considered, I would say we're on the threshold of an exciting new age in strategic planning. ❖

~ X ~

KEEPING CURRENT

❧

The title of this little column is "Keeping Current," which for planners and other futurists means always being slightly ahead. That is no small feat in a time of unpredictability. Now that Newton, Locke, and Skinner are dead, we can never be sure. There are swirling currents everywhere—counter and cross. And the speed. The disorienting speed. Soon mere velocity may of force render even the concept of future impossible.

If there is to be a future that any of us will recognize, four issues must be settled quickly. Questions actually. Questions to which we have no answers because they have not been asked by this generation, nor the one before that, nor the one before that. In fact, the questions usually launch a new epoch. But the questions are fundamental to our world now:

(1) What is the nature of human being?

(2) What is the nature of human systems?

(3) What is the definition of wealth?

(4) What is the meaning of knowledge?

The current search for *human being* ranges from pathetic travesty to the most profound tragedy, often finding both together. From emotionally pornographic talk shows to inane books that typecast the sexes by planetary origin to crack houses within the shadows of steeples, from mysticism to positivism to new-age humanism—the search goes on. Yet, for some reason we have not been of a mind to confront, much less settle, the questions within the question:

(a) Are people good?

(b) Is every person morally responsible?

(c) Is there purpose to life?

(d) Is everyone intelligent?

When and how these and other basic questions are answered is the future.

It is a fascination to watch the current mêlée about *systems*. Curiously,

162

system devotées fall naturally along two sides of a universal divide. On one side are those who rapturously celebrate the advent of "new science" (for the fourth time) with its inexplicable mysteries of the quanta and the blinding clarity of natural laws. On the other side are those who are desperately attempting to extend the systems of the present obsolescence into permanent globalized artifacts of busyness. But systems have their own imperatives:

(1) formations comprise, constructs are composed;

(2) controls free;

(3) the only source of energy is entelechy; and

(4) everything is ruled by the same mean.

Until these principles are appropriated, the future will remain lost in the cliché of "vision"—either delusion or hallucination.

The currency of material *wealth* is pursuit. Its only measure, more. By that measure there is always a balance—a ledger as it were—in which gain is precisely offset by loss. When wealth is "created," as suggested by Adam Smith, et al, the balance becomes imbalance. ("The poor you have with you always.") Mr. Smith was too grounded to foresee capitalism turned inside out by corporations and socialism turned downside up by government—the one looting and pillaging in a battlefield devoid of morality, the other getting and spending as if there were no yesterday because there is no tomorrow. In this world, wealth and debt are the same, and there is no relationship between worth and value. We never imagined that we would see nations, companies, families, and individuals consume themselves with wealth. But we have come to understand diminishing return.

Very soon we shall hear talk of new definitions of wealth. And the lasting conversations will be simply the acknowledgement of the supremacy of people over things. The coin of the realm will be:

(1) wealth as being, not possessing;

(2) wealth as generative, not generated; and

(3) wealth as the common good, not the goods of individuals.

It may be the greatest irony of all time: rationalistic science makes *knowledge* tentative, virtually impossible. So we are never sure of anything. To compensate for lack of knowledge, we have multiplied information. Although we are confused, we are well informed. Maybe we are confused because we are informed. Traditionally, information is inversely proportional to knowledge. But current information is relative to nothing except its own form or, more recently, its own formlessness. Nets, webs, superhighways inform the teeming vacuum of cyberspace, itself indefinable. Data bases are the only reality. T.S. Eliot saw it coming: "Where is the knowledge we lost in information?"

Yet we are on the brink of a great discovery; that is, infinite information means the same as no information. Only then will we be disposed to accept the knowledge implicit in wisdom:

(1) how we know and what we know are the same;

(2) nothing has meaning except in context; and

(3) knowledge exists only in *praxis*.

I think this should keep us current for a while. The present is always in the future. ❖

~ XI ~

The Age of Reform
1971-1996

❧

It was one of these meetings in which a group of educators—all serious-minded and each with some national reputation—sit around a big table and try to foresee the future. Quite actually, that was the assignment: "Scan the horizon and see if you can detect any new educational trends, circumstances, personalities, or philosophies looming there. The basic tactic seemed well advised: anticipation equals preparedness. I had not really expected this future search to yield very much that was either revelatory or edifying. So I was not prepared for what they (we) discovered. Far beyond revelation, it was inspiring. More than edifying, it was absolutely invigorating—rejuvenating.

After an hour or so of intense scanning—each in studied silence, struggling, squinting, and twisting about, trying to achieve focus through the impenetrable mists—everyone declared, much to their collective astonishment, that they had all seen the same thing: nothing.

For several months before the delicate seance, I had been increasingly aware—or so I thought—of what had to be the signs of the turning of ages. And this rather naive exercise in forecasting was enough to confirm my perceptions. There is no other way to see our current situation: The age of reform is history. I didn't share this blinding flash with the others at the meeting. I simply left early, trying not to smile.

Consider the implications—wondrous and wonderful—of the end of reform. Beginning now, there will be, for example:

• No more restructuring, reinventing, or re-engineering
• No more improvement, continuous, or otherwise
• No more participatory management
• No more management

165

- No more leadership theories
- No more paradigm shifts
- No more corporation organization
- No more consensus-building
- No more teaming, councils, or committees
- No more reform legislation
- No more reform wizards, politicians, or evangelists.

In short, it means that anything—idea or terminology—associated with reform is instantly obsolete. No more prefix "re."

Historically and philosophically, reform was (is) the institution's answer to revolution. The abbreviated version of the latest reform movement goes like this: The decade of the 1960s was a virtual explosion of ideas—radical, anti-establishment, irrelevant. No order, no system went unchallenged. But the institution—whose only rationale for existence is self-perpetuation—fought back. And the odds were on its side: inertia (unmoving things stay unmoved); cowardice (talk is cheap); and impotence (gratification overcomes conviction). Furthermore, the institution enticed away the revolutionary fervor by calling up the two postulates of rationalism: (1) all human systems can be perfected; and (2) all human systems deserve to be perfected. The corollary is: progress is made only by incremental improvement. Those ideas, taken together, constituted the dominant philosophy of the American society for the latter half of the 20th century. So, revolution was lost in reform—reform predicated on lies.

Probably anyone reading this essay has lived all of his or her life in the age of reform and is captivated by reform mentality. No wonder we have forgotten the original intent of reform—the good of human beings. And instead, we have somehow agreed to serve existing systems, willingly sacrifice the person to them. Economically, we have created systems of scarcity; politically, systems of dependence; socially, systems of conflict; religiously, systems of exploitation; educationally, systems of abject servitude to capitalism. The perverse effect is always the legacy of reform.

There is one fundamental principle that all reform ignores; that is, nothing can be *better* unless it is *good*. So it should be with no regret that we now acknowledge that our existing systems are not good, abandon them with extreme urgency, and create new systems designed to serve human beings—systems of continuous creation. The first step in creation is destruction.

When reformers look into the future, they see nothing. When creators see the future, it becomes a new reality. ❖

SELECTED BIBLIOGRAPHY

Andrews, Kenneth R. *The Concept of Corporate Strategy*. Homewood, Illinois: Richard Irwin, Inc., 1980.

Bean, J. P., and G. D. Kuh. "A Typology of Planning Problems." *Journal of Higher Education* (55/1, 1984): 36-51.

Bennis, Warren. *On Becoming a Leader*. Reading, Massachusetts: Perseus Books, 1989.

Bennis, Warren. *Why Leaders Can't Lead*. San Francisco: Jossey-Bass Publishers, 1990.

Bennis, Warren and Burt Nanus. *Leaders: Strategies for Taking Charge*. New York: HarperCollins, 1985.

Brandenburger, Adam M. and Barry J. Nalebuff. *Co-opetition*. New York: Doubleday, 1996.

Bridges, William. *Jobshift*. Reading, Massachusetts: Perseus Books, 1995.

Caldwell, P. "Some Better Ideas from Ford Motors C.E.O." *Planning Review* (September 1984): 8-9.

Carse, James. *Breakfast at the Victory: The Mysticism of Ordinary Experience*. San Francisco: Harper Books, 1994.

Costa, Arthur L. and Rosemarie M. Liebmann (Editors). *The Process-Centered School*. Thousand Oaks, California: Corwin Press, Inc., 1997.

Covey, Stephen R. *Principle-Centered Leadership*. New York: Summit Book, 1990.

Cribben, James. *Effective Managerial Leadership*. New York: American Management Association, Inc., 1972.

Donnelly, J. H., J. L. Gibson, and J. M. Ivancevich. *Fundamentals of Management*. Plano, Texas: Business Publications, 1984.

Duckworth, A., and R. Kranyik. "What Business Are We In?" *The School Administrator* (August 1984): 6-8.

Drucker, Peter F. *The Practice of Management*. New York: Harper & Row, Publishers, Inc., 1954.

Drucker, Peter. *Concept of the Corporation*. New York: John Day Company, 1946.

Ellis, Darryl J., and Peter P. Pekar, Jr. *Planning for Nonplanners: Planning Basics for Managers*. New York: AMACOM, 1980.

Famularo, Joseph J. *Organization Planning Manual, Revised Edition*. New York: AMACOM, 1979.

Frankl, Viktor. *Man's Search for Meaning*. Boston: Beacon Press, 1992.

Gardner, John W. "Leaders and Followers." *Liberal Education* (March-April 1987): 14.

Gates, Henry Louis. "The End of Loyalty." *The New Yorker* (March 9, 1998): 34.

Glavin, G. "The Management of Planning: A Third Dimension of Business Planning." *The Business Quarterly* (Autumn 1974): 43-51.

Gortner, Harold F., Julianne Mahler, and Jeanne Bell Nicholson. *Organization Theory*. Chicago, Illinois: The Dorsey Press, 1987.

Grossman, Lee. *The Change Agent*. New York: AMACOM, 1974.

Hayman, J. "Relationship of Strategic Planning and Future Methodologies." Paper presented at the annual meeting of the American Educational Research Association, Los Angeles, California (April 1981).

Heider, John. *The Tao of Leadership*. New York: Bantam Books, 1985.

Humboldt, Wilhelm. *The Sphere and Duties of Government*. Bristol, England: Thoemmes Press, 1996.

Houston, P. "Involve Your Community in Planning for It." *The School Administrator* (August 1984): 11-13.

Kastens, Merritt L. *Long-Range Planning for Your Business*. New York: AMACOM, 1976.

Kaufman, Roger and Jerry Herman. *Strategic Planning in Education*. Lancaster, Pennsylvania: Technomic Publishing Co., 1991.

Kay, Emanuel. *The Crisis in Middle Management*. New York: AMACOM, 1974.

Korton, David C. *When Corporations Rule the World*. West Hartford, Connecticut: Kumarian Press, Inc., 1995.

Land, George and Beth Jarman. *Break-point and Beyond*. New York: HarperBusiness, 1992.

Seth Lubove, "Get'em Before They Get You." *Forbes* (July 31, 1995): 8.

Shafritz, Jay M. and J. Steven Ott. *Classics of Organization Theory*. Belmont, California: Wadsworth Publishing Company, 1996.

Simon, Herbert A. "The Proverbs of Administration." *Public Administration Review* (Winter 1946): 53-67.

Mintzberg, Henry. *The Rise and Fall of Strategic Planning*. New York: Free Press, 1993.

Mueller, Ronald E., and David H. Moore. "America's Blind Spot: Industrial Policy." *Challenge* (January/February 1982): 5-13.

Naor, Jacob. "Strategic Planning Under Resource Constraints." *Business* (September/October 1981): 15-19.

Naylor, Thomas H. *Strategic Planning Management*. Oxford, Ohio: Planning Executives Institute, 1980.

Neill, S. "Planning for the Future." *Planning for Tomorrow's Schools* (1983): 7-30.

Ouchi, William G. *Theory Z*. New York: Avon Books, 1981.

Reich, Robert. *The Work of Nations*. New York: Random House, 1992.

Samuelson, Robert J. "Crackpot Prophet." *Newsweek* (March 10, 1997): 50.

Shlain, Leonard. *The Alphabet Versus the Goddess*. New York: Penguin Group, 1998.

Soros, George. "The Capitalistic Threat." *Atlantic Monthy* (February 1997): 47-48.

Steiner, G. *Strategic Planning*. New York: The Free Press, 1979.

Thurow, Lester. *The Future Capitalism*. New York: William Murrow and Company, 1996.

Tichy, Noel M. and Mary Anne DeVanna. *The Transformational Leader*. New York: John Wiley and Sons, 1986.

Tita, M., and R. Allio. "3M's Strategy System—Planning in an Innovative Corporation." *Planning Review* (September 1984): 10-15.

Wood, K., and S. Wood. "Are Corporate Strategic Planning Techniques Useful in Public Higher Education?" Paper presented at the Joint Conference of the Southern Association for Institutional Research and the North Carolina Association for Institutional Research, Charlotte, NC (October 1981).

Zukav, Gary. *The Dancing Wu Li Masters*. New York: Bantam Books, 1979.

 All of our programs are designed with these purposes: to develop the capability of our clients to participate in the facilitation of their own plans, to extend the process throughout their schools, and to sustain the experience of continuous creation. All programs carry graduate credit through the University System of Maryland, as well as provide continuing support from Cambridge Associates, the program reference manual, and an introduction into an extensive network of other districts utilizing the Cambridge strategic planning process and discipline.

❧ STRATEGIC THINKING

IN PREPARATION OF PLANNING...

Strategic thinking means seeing in different ways. This program will enable you to prepare your organization for planning before the activity actually begins; identify leaders within your organization necessary for the planning effort; and recognize the need for system and individual capacities that will ensure the plan is realized. The five arenas of strategic thinking are examined in depth.

❧ STRATEGIC PLANNING

DEVELOPING THE PLAN...

This program will equip you to facilitate your organization's strategic planning process; apply the Cambridge planning discipline; establish locus of control within the system, rather than reacting to external factors; stimulate positive community involvement and support; and develop the organizational capability for continuous creation. Participants are provided with continuing support by Cambridge staff and are introduced to a network of local facilitators.

❧ STRATEGIC ACTION

REALIZING THE PLAN...

This program will enable you to understand the critical relationship between strategic intent and action; learn how to meaningful appropriate different kinds of action; explore a completely new concept of organization; build capacity in action; and create an organizational culture that focuses all energies on the mission and objectives.

❧ STRATEGIC ORGANIZATION

ORGANIZING THROUGH ACTION...

This program will enable you actually to create an organizational formation capable of realizing the plan; establish a process of transition from traditional organization to whole-context organization; localize and personalize all "jobs" in the system; put in place a generative evaluation methodology; and establish mutual expectations and commitments for everyone within the system.

❧ SCHOOL PLANNING

SCHOOL PLANNING IN A STRATEGIC CONTEXT...

This program will enable you to understand the linkage of school plans to the district plan; recognize the uniqueness of the site and its special place within the system; develop implementable site plans; learn how site planning will allow you to comply with state mandates for school improvement plans; and learn how site planning can be integrated with regional accreditation.

All programs may be delivered locally. For a complete list of programs, including dates, locations and costs, please call (800) 343-4590 or visit our web site at www.colonialcambridge.com

Products All products listed below can be ordered by calling (800) 343-4590, faxing your order with a purchase order number to (334) 279-7151, or visiting our website at www.colonialcambridge.com.

BOOKS BY COOK

Strategics®: The Art and Science of Holistic Strategy

AUTHOR: WILLIAM J. COOK, JR. © 2000, 305 PAGES
GREENWOOD PUBLISHING / CONNECTICUT • LONDON
CALL TO ORDER (800) 225-5800 OR www.greenwood.com

 This book is about Strategics®, not as the idea is currently interpreted and applied in corporate strategy, but as the only human power with the potential of radically transforming existing organizations into systems of continuous creation. In its full expression, Strategics® has three aspects: *Thinking, Planning, and Action.*

Although strategic issues may change from time to time, *Strategic Thinking* will always embrace five arenas: the definition of strategy; the meaning of leaders and leading; the distinction between condition and cause; and nature of systems; and the characteristics of organization.

The recent popularity of *Strategic Planning* as a management practice has all but obscured the original concept, and, consequently, has diminished its effect on human systems. The only definition that captures the original intent is: *Strategic Planning is the means by which a community of people create artifactual systems to serve extraordinary purpose.*

Strategic Action defines the three kinds of action and explains how each can be instrumental in realizing the plan in two ways: by conforming organization to action and by systemizing all action. The result is that organizations can go far beyond merely improving that which already exists. They can actually create new systems that are capable of constant emergence—always vital, always creative.

The Evolving Corporation: A Humanistic Interpretation

AUTHOR: WILLIAM J. COOK, JR. © 2000, 325 PAGES
GREENWOOD PUBLISHING / CONNECTICUT • LONDON
CALL TO ORDER (800) 225-5800 OR www.greenwood.com

 The modern corporation, which has been the dominant organization of Western civilization, inevitably is being replaced by a new system of human organization that correspondingly reflects the changing aspects of that society.

The purpose of this book is to trace the historical and philosophical development of the corporation-model organization, to offer a critical analysis of the modern corporation, and to suggest the dimensions and dynamics of the emerging organizations.

This book is a challenge to the corporation-model organization in three ways: it reveals the corporation as a rationalistic contradiction of religion and science that is impossible to sustain; it argues that the contemporary corporation is fundamentally adverse to both the individual and society; it proposes an alternative organization that is exclusively and only dedicated to the common good.

Strategic Planning for America's Schools

AUTHOR: WILLIAM J. COOK, JR. © 2001, 173 PAGES
THE CAMBRIDGE GROUP
CALL TO ORDER (800) 343-4590

This best-selling book has been completely updated and refined to enhance your understanding of the discipline and process of strategic planning. Discover how strategic planning can enable you to create a brighter educational future for the students in your district or school system. It is the definitive work on strategic planning for education.

MONOGRAPHS

The Urgency of Change: The Metamorphosis of America's Schools
AUTHOR: BILL COOK © 1996, 40 PAGES

Creating Schools for Planning
AUTHOR: HOWARD FEDDEMA © 1994, 20 PAGES

Sartor Resartus
AUTHOR: BILL COOK © 1992, 20 PAGES

Implementing Site-Based Planning in Small School Districts
AUTHORS: WILLIAM D. BRECK AND SUSAN VIROSTEK © 1992, 24 PAGES

VIDEO CASSETTE SERIES
STRATEGICS® for Education

A comprehensive three-tape video series, narrated by Dr. Bill Cook, reveals powerful components of STRATEGIC THINKING, STRATEGIC PLANNING, and STRATEGIC ACTION, which can be used for your in-service training program.

STRATEGIC THINKING © 1996, 44 minutes
- *Introduction to Strategics®*
- *The Nature of Systems*

STRATEGIC PLANNING © 1996, 88 minutes
- *The Discipline of the Plan*
- *The Process of Planning*

STRATEGIC ACTION © 1996, 31 minutes
- *Creating the Organization Design through Mutual Expectations*
- *Systemizing the Action through Site Planning*

REFERENCE MANUALS
Action Team Leader's Guide

This guide has evolved over several years as Cambridge facilitators worked with action team leaders in over 700 organizations. Written in the second person, it is intended to offer practical, step-by-step assistance in dealing with the issues and concerns faced most often by team leaders. Since the development of action plans is the most important phase of planning, not even the smallest detail can be left to chance. And beyond that, the credibility of the entire plan depends on the action plans. This manual details action team orientation, development, benefits, activities, outlines of team meetings, and includes hand-outs and reference material for reproduction.

Strategic & Site Planning Workbooks

These workbooks are helpful tools for districts beginning their planning process. It defines the elements in the strategic and site planning disciplines and includes examples of each with additional workspace for participants. It also contains forms used in the initial planning process.

Facilitator's Guide for Strategic Planning

This reference manual has been used to train over 4,000 facilitators in Cambridge's extensive Strategic Planning program. It contains the process and discipline that has been used to facilitate

over 700 Strategic Plans in Educational Systems around the world.